CAMPAIGN 427

KINGS MOUNTAIN 1780

The Tide Turns in the South

DAVID SMITH ILLUSTRATED BY GRAHAM TURNER

OSPREY PUBLISHING
Bloomsbury Publishing Plc
Kemp House, Chawley Park, Cumnor Hill, Oxford OX2 9PH, UK
29 Earlsfort Terrace, Dublin 2, Ireland
Bloomsbury Publishing Inc.
1359 Broadway, 12th Floor, New York, NY 10018, USA
E-mail: info@ospreypublishing.com
www.ospreypublishing.com

OSPREY is a trademark of Osprey Publishing Ltd

First published in Great Britain in 2026

© Osprey Publishing Ltd, 2026

All rights reserved. No part of this publication may be reproduced or transmitted in any form or by any means, electronic or mechanical, including photocopying, recording, or any information storage or retrieval system, without prior permission in writing from the publisher; or ii) used or reproduced in any way for the training, development or operation of artificial intelligence (AI) technologies, including generative AI technologies. The rights holders expressly reserve this publication from the text and data mining exception as per Article 4(3) of the Digital Single Market Directive (EU) 2019/790.

A catalog record for this book is available from the British Library.

ISBN: PB 9781472870476; eBook 9781472870445; ePDF 9781472870452; XML 9781472870469

26 27 28 29 30   10 9 8 7 6 5 4 3 2 1

Maps by Bounford.com
3D BEV by Paul Kime
Index by Angela Hall
Typeset by Lumina Datamatics Ltd
Printed by Repro India Ltd

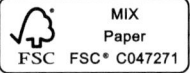

Acknowledgments

I would like to thank Robert C. Holmes, Park Ranger at the Kings Mountain National Military Park, for his invaluable help in the preparation of this book. His insights and comments were extremely helpful and any errors that remain are entirely of my own making.

I would also like to thank my editor at Osprey, Brianne Bellio, for her support and, as always, give a salute to Graham Turner for turning my sparse descriptions into the beautiful color plates that grace this book.

Artist's note

Readers may care to note that the original paintings from which the colour plates in this book were prepared are available for private sale. All reproduction copyright whatsoever is retained by the publishers. All enquiries should be addressed to:

Graham Turner, PO Box 568, Aylesbury, Bucks, HP17 8EX, UK
www.studio88.co.uk

The publishers regret that they can enter into no correspondence upon this matter.

Osprey Publishing supports the Woodland Trust, the UK's leading woodland conservation charity.

To find out more about our authors and books visit www.ospreypublishing.com. Here you will find extracts, author interviews, details of forthcoming events and the option to sign up for our newsletter.

For product safety related questions contact productsafety@bloomsbury.com

Front cover main illustration: The charge of the provincials at Kings Mountain, October 7, 1780. (Graham Turner)
Title page image: "The Gathering of the Overmountain Men at Sycamore Shoals," by Lloyd Branson. (Lloyd Branson (painter), public domain, via Wikimedia Commons)

CONTENTS

ORIGINS OF THE CAMPAIGN 5

CHRONOLOGY 8

OPPOSING COMMANDERS 10
Loyalist . Patriot

OPPOSING FORCES 14
Loyalist . Patriot . Order of battle

OPPOSING PLANS 22
Loyalist . Patriot

THE CAMPAIGN 25
The destruction of Gates' Grand Army . Cornwallis' offensive . The Siege of Mackay's Trading Post . Ferguson's campaign begins . The muster at Sycamore Shoals . The final reinforcements . The battle

AFTERMATH 85

THE BATTLEFIELD TODAY 89

SELECT BIBLIOGRAPHY 93

INDEX 95

British expansion into the backcountry, June–August 1780

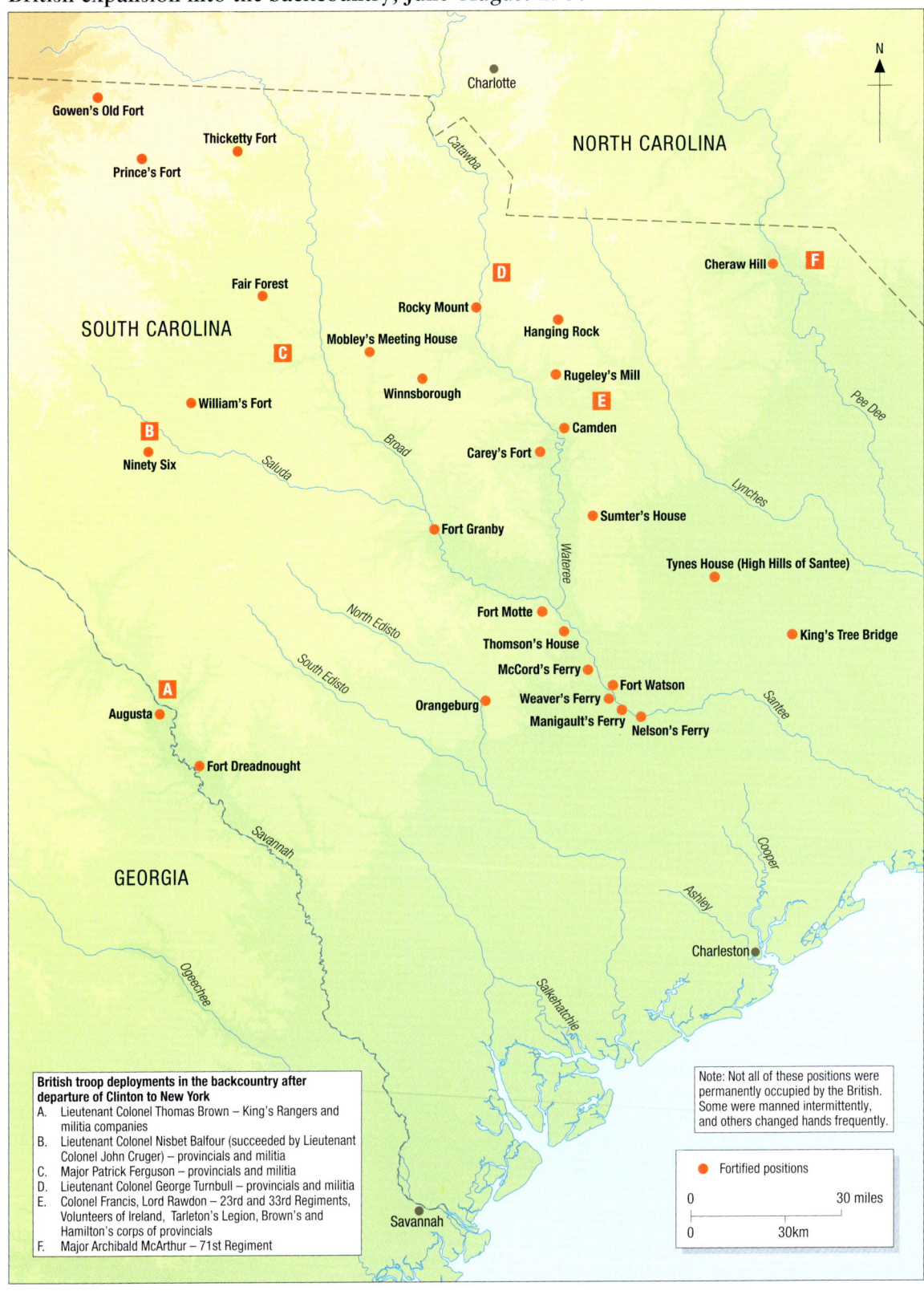

ORIGINS OF THE CAMPAIGN

Following the fall of Charleston, the British strategy in the South appeared to be working smoothly. The main American army in the region had been neutralized, and the British felt able to move onto the next phase of their plan – the subjugation of the backcountry.

Referring to the area roughly 50 miles inland from the coast and stretching all the way to the Appalachian Mountains (often referred to as the Blue Ridge or Smoky Mountains), the backcountry was a mixture of plains and hills, forests, and streams. Game had once been common and varied, but both bison and elk had been hunted to extinction in the region by the time the British arrived to reassert their dominance.

Two ethnic groups were most common: Scots-Irish, with a reputation for having a fiery temperament; and Germans, who were regarded as quieter and more sociable. Slavery was a fact of life in the region, and around 10 percent of the population were enslaved.

It was an isolated, mostly lawless land, with no love for religion. "In the back parts of Carolina," noted Major George Hanger when he looked back on his days of service there, "you might search after an angel with as much chance of finding one as a parson; there is no such thing."

Alcohol consumption was prodigious. Rye whiskey, cider, rum, and brandy made from either apples or pears all did the job, while the more restrained among the population drank beer.

The historian Ian Saberton, who has written extensively on the war during this period, captured the mood of the region, where there was little sense of a "coming together" to form one nation out of many. "Not a melting pot," he explained, "the backcountry was more akin to the Tower of Babel."

Taming such a territory would be a formidable task. Britain's plan was to enlist Loyalist supporters to form their own militia battalions, which could then act as a sort of police force for the region, to keep a lid on Patriot

"South-Carolina and parts adjacent; shewing the movements of the American and British armies," by David Ramsay, published 1785. (Library of Congress, Geography and Map Division)

activity, encourage more Loyalists to declare themselves in support of the Crown, and free up the regular army for operations elsewhere. On paper, it seemed like a reasonable strategy, but, in reality, it was flawed, and British actions further undermined the premise. This was not a chess board, where a piece could play no more part in the contest once removed. The Americans were able to constantly generate new pieces, in the shape of militia units and a reformed regular army.

The British also displayed a lack of finesse. It was vital to instill confidence in Loyalists without antagonizing neutrals – this was a delicate balancing act, but they never mastered it. In fact, a decision by the British commander-in-chief, Sir Henry Clinton, was disastrous in this respect. Having previously allowed civilians to simply stay out of the war, a declaration of June 3, 1780 forced them to pick a side. Those who did not actively support the British in their efforts to restore control over the colony would be considered enemies. Thousands of men who had surrendered at Charleston, who may have considered their war over, were now provoked into taking up arms against the British once more.

Another factor that weakened the British in the region was the return of Clinton to New York shortly after issuing this incendiary proclamation. He took 4,500 men with him, leaving Charles, Earl Cornwallis in command with just 6,500 men in South Carolina. Cornwallis would receive a welcome gift when Horatio Gates marched directly into a pitched battle at Camden and was completely routed, but with many posts to hold they were forced to spread themselves thinly.

The Loyalists were therefore essential to pad out British numbers. Recruitment of units had been discouraged while American resistance was tackled at Charleston, but after the fall of the city, Clinton had given authorization for a concerted effort to raise and train units. Key in this effort was a Scottish officer of some renown – Major Patrick Ferguson.

The British commander-in-chief, Sir Henry Clinton, left the South in a precarious position when he took 4,500 men back to New York in June 1780. (Prints, Drawings and Watercolors from the Anne S. K. Brown Military Collection, Brown Digital Repository, Brown University Library)

Ferguson's orders were simple. He was to enlist "all of the young or unmarried men of the provinces of Georgia and the two Carolinas, as opportunity shall offer, to serve under the orders of Lt General Earl Cornwallis or other general officer commanding in these provinces. This militia you will form into companies consisting of from 50 to 100 men each and will, when the local and other circumstances will admit of it, form battalions consisting of from 6 to 12 companies each..." Older men, or those with families, were not considered suitable for offensive operations, but could be organized into companies for home defense if the need arose.

Three bodies of troops had been ordered into the backcountry following the fall of Charleston. Ferguson, at the head of 600 men, had made for the British post at Ninety Six. The commanding officer there, Nisbet Balfour, had little confidence in Ferguson and said as much to Cornwallis, who took the advice to heart and reined Ferguson in.

"I agree, sir, perfectly," he wrote to Ferguson on June 2, "that it is absolutely necessary to regulate the militia of the province and am now busied in forming a plan for that purpose. As soon as I have been able to compleat [*sic*] it, I will transmit it to you. In the mean time I must desire that you will take no steps in this business without receiving directions from me."

Ferguson bowed to Cornwallis' wishes, but he also took steps to demonstrate that Clinton had already authorized him to act. Writing to Cornwallis in respectful terms ("I shall pay the most implicit obedience") he also, pointedly, included a copy of Clinton's detailed instructions.

This kind of internecine discord was not the most promising way for the next stage of the British plan to open, but the hold-up was brief. By June 8, Cornwallis was writing again. No copy of this letter has survived, but Ferguson replied quickly, and it is clear that the message contained Cornwallis' instructions for the raising of militia. Ferguson was in business, and he was optimistic about both the numbers of men he could raise, and their quality. He saw no problem in recruiting a force that would require minimal support in pacifying the entire region.

In a letter to Cornwallis he wrote, "it appears to me that the loyalists… will be very sufficient with two or three small detachments to secure this country…" His optimism appeared boundless as he went on: "there will be a militia in this province soon form'd… much more numerous and ten times more to be trusted than any the rebels ever turn'd out."

That boast would be put to the test.

Ferguson went on to raise around 4,000 Loyalist militia, but simply recruiting, training, and supplying them was a huge undertaking, and the question would remain as to how they stacked up against their opponents. Patriot militia had already proved it could do the job the British were hoping for from their Loyalists – subduing the population in the absence of regular forces. Could the Loyalists be as effective?

The question would soon attain critical importance because patience was not going to be the British watchword. Before South Carolina had been fully pacified, Cornwallis decided to take the offensive once more, marching his regular troops into North Carolina. The Loyalists under Ferguson would be counted on to keep the South Carolina backcountry under control, but it appeared he was the only British officer who had genuine confidence in them.

The fall of Charleston, after a lengthy siege, opened up the South Carolina backcountry for the British. Painting by Alonzo Chappel. (Prints, Drawings and Watercolors from the Anne S. K. Brown Military Collection, Brown Digital Repository, Brown University Library)

CHRONOLOGY

1780

May 29	Banastre Tarleton destroys Abraham Buford's command at Waxhaws.
June 8	Thomas Brown occupies Augusta.
June 20	Loyalists rise prematurely and are routed at the Battle of Ramsour's Mill.
July 12	Patriot victory at the Battle of Williamson's Plantation ("Huck's Defeat").
July 30	Thicketty Fort (aka Fort Anderson) is captured by Shelby.
	Sumter launches a bold attack at Rocky Mount.
	Successful surprise attack on the British garrison at Hanging Rock.
August 6	Sumter and Davie launch a larger-scale attack at Hanging Rock.
August 8	Ambush of British forces by Elijah Clarke at Wofford's Iron Works.
August 16	Battle of Camden – Gates' army annihilated by Cornwallis.
August 18	Tarleton catches Sumter napping at Fishing Creek.
August 19	Shelby, Clarke, and Williams inflict a sharp defeat on British forces at Musgrove Mill (some sources state this took place on August 18).
August 25	Francis Marion frees Continental Army prisoners at Nelson's Ferry.
September 4	Marion ambushes Micajah Ganey at Blue Savannah.
September 14–18	Thomas Brown holds out for four days at the Siege of Mackay's Trading Post.
September 26	British enter Charlotte, North Carolina.

The Kings Mountain campaign

September 1	Ferguson rejoins his command after receiving orders from Cornwallis.
September 2	Ferguson's corps begins its march.
September 7	Ferguson crosses the border into North Carolina.
September 9	Proclamation issued to the Overmountain Men.
September 12	Indecisive clash with McDowell.
September 25	Overmountain Men muster at Sycamore Shoals.

September 26	Overmountain Men begin their march.
September 30	Ferguson learns of the muster at Sycamore Shoals.
October 1	Patriots reach Quaker Meadows.
October 3	Patriots reach Gilbert Town.
October 6	Ferguson marches his men to Kings Mountain and sets up camp.
	Patriots march to the Cowpens, where they are joined by Hill, Lacey, and Williams. At 2100hrs, the slimmed-down force sets off for Kings Mountain.
October 7	Patriots secure a crushing victory at Kings Mountain.
October 12	Cornwallis abandons Charlotte.

1781

| January 17 | Tarleton defeated at the Battle of Cowpens. |

OPPOSING COMMANDERS

LOYALIST

Respected by his men and his enemies, **Lieutenant General Charles, Earl Cornwallis (1738–1805)** was one of the most effective British commanders of the war, and it is tempting to ponder how he might have wielded the 28,000-strong army of the opening campaign in 1776. By the time he got a command, it numbered just 6,500 and he was operating in the vast territories of Virginia, Georgia, and the Carolinas.

Left to command in the South when Sir Henry Clinton returned to New York following the fall of Charleston, Cornwallis was a naturally aggressive commander who inherited an almost impossible situation. Still, his decision to open an offensive into North Carolina before South Carolina had been fully subdued (although admittedly that might never have happened) stretched British forces too thinly and opened up the possibility of defeat at Kings Mountain.

Cornwallis went on to lead the British to a disastrous defeat at Yorktown, but his reputation was rescued by his ability to cast blame for that on Clinton. Consequently, he was able to rebuild his career, serving as Governor-General in India and Lord Lieutenant of Ireland.

Before his fateful date with Patriot militia at Kings Mountain, **Major Patrick Ferguson (1744–80)** had already won renown for his development of a breech-loading rifle that bore his name. The Ferguson rifle built on an existing design, making it suitable for military use, but faced with the traditionally impassive face of the British Army, he failed to get his excellent weapon authorized for adoption in significant numbers.

A cornet in the Scots Greys at the age of 15, a long and unspecified illness after service during the Seven Years' War left him with a limp – just the first of many tolls his military career would take on his body. A captain in the 70th Regiment's light infantry company by 1774, he attended Major General William Howe's

Charles, Earl Cornwallis, commander of the British forces in the South, was an instinctively aggressive commander. (Prints, Drawings and Watercolors from the Anne S. K. Brown Military Collection, Brown Digital Repository, Brown University Library)

famous light infantry training camp that year and won favor with the man who would command British troops during the first two campaigns of the revolution.

Shot through the elbow at the Battle of the Brandywine in 1777, Ferguson was commanding provincial troops by the time he went south with Clinton in 1780, with the provincial rank of lieutenant colonel. On April 18, 1780, he was made a major in the 71st (Fraser's Highlanders) Regiment, and was appointed Inspector of Militia by Clinton in May of that year.

Usually a thoughtful officer (when based at Grenada he encouraged his men to grow their own vegetables to supplement their diet and promote better health), his ill-judged handling of his small command would ultimately lead to his undoing.

A member of one of the most illustrious families in New York society (his great-grandfather had been a mayor of New York City and also a governor of New York), **Captain Abraham DePeyster (1753–*c*.99)** joined the 4th (King's) American Regiment and was commissioned as a captain in December 1776. He had the local rank of lieutenant colonel at the Battle of Kings Mountain,

Portrait of Patrick Ferguson, commander of the Loyalist forces at Kings Mountain, by Robert Wilson. (Kings Mountain National Military Park)

Abraham DePeyster, second-in-command of the Loyalists at Kings Mountain, had started his military career as a captain in the New York Volunteers. (From The New York Public Library)

No contemporary portrait of William Campbell has survived, but this painting, by Robert Wilson, draws on a reported likeness to his grandson, William Campbell Preston. (Kings Mountain National Military Park)

John Sevier, who brought around 240 men from Washington County, North Carolina, to the mustering point at Sycamore Shoals. (Hulton Archive/Getty Images)

where he acted as second-in-command to Ferguson and offered the surrender of the remainder of the Loyalist force. After the battle, he was held as a prisoner until 1783, when he was exchanged and went to New York in time to be a part of the British evacuation at the end of the war. He then settled in Canada.

Abraham had two younger brothers, Frederick and James, who also served as Loyalist officers, and on at least one occasion Cornwallis appears to have had difficulty telling the brothers apart.

A Yorkshireman by birth, **Lieutenant Colonel Thomas Brown (1750–1825)** emigrated to Georgia in 1774 and remained loyal to the Crown when revolutionary fervor began to mount. Although he declared he had no intention of taking up arms in the struggle, he was assaulted (his skull was fractured by a musket butt), burned, scalped, and then tarred and feathered by a mob of Patriots in August 1775.

After recovering, he became a Loyalist officer and was soon commanding the King's (Carolina) Rangers, taking part in the 1779 Siege of Savannah. Following the war, in recognition of his service, Brown was awarded 8,000 acres of land in the Caribbean.

PATRIOT

Colonel William Campbell (1745–81) would be considered unusually tall today, standing at 6ft 6in, but in an age when the average man stood around 5ft 8in, he was a giant. Although he was only nominally in command of Patriot forces at Kings Mountain, he was an accomplished and experienced officer. Born in Argyll, Scotland, his family moved to Virginia and he fought the Cherokee as a captain of militia before taking part in Lord Dunmore's War in 1774.

Campbell signed the Fincastle Resolutions on January 20, 1775, the first declared statement of hostile intent towards Great Britain, and he won a reputation as a harsh and uncompromising commander – Loyalists called him "the bloody tyrant of Washington County." He was a colonel by the time he led his men to join the gathering Patriot militia on the hunt for Ferguson.

After the battle, he continued to serve and was present at the Battle of Guilford Courthouse. He was promoted to brigadier general in 1781, but died shortly thereafter, apparently of a heart attack.

Lieutenant Colonel John Sevier's (1745–1815) grandfather was a French immigrant, while his father had been born in England and his mother was from the Shenandoah Valley. He worked as a farmer, trader, and surveyor, also serving as a militia officer, and moved to the Tennessee Valley in the 1770s, becoming a magistrate in the Watauga Association.

The British were not high on the list of problems for the region, and Sevier was among a small band of militia who withstood a two-week siege by Cherokee forces at Fort Caswell in 1776. By 1777, he was a lieutenant colonel in the Washington County Regiment from North Carolina and was a prominent figure in the backcountry when the British attempted to take control.

In 1784, Sevier was involved in the setting up of an independent state, Franklin, which had ambitions to become the 14th member of the United States, but it only lasted until 1788. He later served as the first governor of Tennessee.

Born in Maryland, **Colonel Isaac Shelby (1750–1826)** had Welsh roots and gained his first taste of military experience as a lieutenant in the Virginia militia during Lord Dunmore's War, earning praise for his conduct at the Battle of Point Pleasant (October 10, 1774).

Shelby was surveying land in Kentucky when news of the fall of Charleston reached him, and he was soon commanding militiamen in South Carolina. In July 1780, he captured the garrison of Thicketty Fort without firing a shot and was then drawn into the pursuit of Ferguson.

After the Battle of Kings Mountain, Shelby took the field again in operations against Cornwallis, culminating in the British capitulation at Yorktown. In later life, he twice served as governor of Kentucky.

A swashbuckling character, **Lieutenant Colonel Elijah Clarke (1742–99)**, or "Clark" as he is often referred to, featured in a number of skirmishes, notably at Kettle Creek (February 14, 1779), and twice suffered wounds in battle. His attack on Mackay's Trading Post (rather grandly referred to as "the First Siege of Augusta") revealed a daring side, and he also took part in a more successful second siege the following year.

After the war, Clarke saw action as an "Indian fighter," served as a major general in the French Army, and established an independent state, the "Trans-Oconee Republic" in 1794 – a hare-brained scheme that did not last long but did nothing to dent Clarke's popularity as a Revolutionary War hero.

Isaac Shelby, depicted here in later life as governor of Kentucky. (Sepia Times/Universal Images Group via Getty Images)

Elijah Clarke had given his parole to the British, but was convinced to take up arms against them once more. (Granger NYC/Topfoto)

OPPOSING FORCES

LOYALIST

The British had been stung by relying on Southern Loyalist militia before. Back in 1776, an uprising was planned to coincide with the arrival of an expeditionary force commanded by Clinton, but the Loyalists jumped the gun and were soundly defeated at Moore's Creek Bridge, in North Carolina, before the supporting British regulars arrived. This time, it was hoped that order would prevail – specifically British orders. Patrick Ferguson was to raise, equip, and train Loyalists, forming disciplined units that could be relied upon in battle.

Aware that some men would be suspicious of being tricked into a long-term enlistment, Clinton had instructed Ferguson to give each recruit a written certificate, stating (in part), "I hereby certify that AB has joined the British Army as a militia man, and not as a regular soldier, and has only engaged to serve any six months of the ensuing twelve that may be required... I further certify that he... is not obliged under any pretence [*sic*] to march beyond North Carolina or Georgia..."

Despite the intention of proceeding along a very formal route towards the raising of companies, spontaneous gatherings continued. At Orangeburg, an "association" of Loyalists had formed and Ferguson was quick to put an official stamp upon it. On June 12, he traveled to a meeting of the men and informed them of the militia arrangements in place, in order to produce a "more regular association." These arrangements appear to have been acceptable to most of the men, as 294 of them signed up. British authority

The Battle of Moore's Creek Bridge by Gil Cohen, from the Moore's Creek National Battleground Park. (Tango Images/Alamy)

was not blind and unyielding – Ferguson noted that the men were allowed to disapprove of certain individuals joining the regiment, and each company chose its own officers.

Cornwallis expressed his satisfaction regarding this start to the forming of a Loyalist force, and admitted to Ferguson that he (Ferguson) had "engaged in a most troublesome business, but in my opinion a most important one."

By June 23, men were "flocking to him from all parts of the country," according to the diary of his aide, Lieutenant Anthony Allaire, and they finally numbered around 4,000 – although not all of these were eligible for offensive campaigning and he had nowhere near that number with him in the run-up to Kings Mountain. In fact, there is some debate on exactly how many men Ferguson had with him during the battle. It is generally accepted that he had around 1,100 under his command (the nephew of Abraham DePeyster gave a presentation in 1881 in which he disputed that figure, but his arguments were complicated).

With around 100 provincial troops from the American Volunteers, 450 North Carolina Loyalist militia, 350 South Carolina Loyalist militia, 35 men from Colonel Richard King's regiment, and a few wagoners, he most likely had around 1,000 to 1,100 officers and men under his command on the day of the battle. It is possible that a number of men, possibly as many as 200, were on foraging duty when the Patriot force attacked.

As well as the number, the quality of the men is also debatable. In August, Ferguson was lamenting the tendency of his militia to come and go as they pleased. The young, single men, who made the best soldiers, were the most likely to disappear on a whim (Ferguson referred to them as "giddy young men") and keeping these part-time soldiers focused was a serious problem. Famously, Ferguson controlled his men in battle with the help of a whistle. Although this brought disparaging comments from some, who saw it as undignified and even comical, it was at least an effort towards establishing order in the chaos of battle.

Patriot forces close in on Ferguson's postion at Kings Mountain in this 19th-century illustration by F. C. Yohn. (North Wind Picture Archives/Alamy)

It is unclear if Ferguson had any of his famous rifles with him at Kings Mountain. They had been placed in storage after he was injured at the Battle of the Brandywine in 1777, and although there is a note that 100 rifles were sent to Ferguson's corps in the South, it is unclear if they were of his own design.

PATRIOT

Patriot militia were used to operating in small bands, but they had already shown they could mass with telling effect at Saratoga in 1777. In the South, the Patriots could move quickly and hit hard, and the string of minor engagements and skirmishes involving them grew longer every month. For the Battle of Kings Mountain, a number of these smaller units came together, but there is a little confusion over exactly how many made it to the final battleground.

The core of the little army was formed when John Sevier and Isaac Shelby pledged to come together to face the threat posed by Ferguson. Settlers from over the mountains had largely been unconcerned by the war; they were more preoccupied with disputes with the Native tribes upon whose lands they were living. That does not mean they had not been active before – Charles McDowell had previously called for riflemen from over the mountains, and they would make a telling contribution, especially at Musgrove Mill, but the Kings Mountain campaign was to mark their biggest impact on the war.

The term "Overmountain Men" was not in use at the time, having been adopted by historians after the events in question. Ferguson referred to them as "Back-Water" or "Back Mountain" men, and his second-in-command, Abraham DePeyster, called them "the yelling boys." Whatever they were called, they were formidable individuals, but not used to operating in large groups under the command of officers. The men who met at Sycamore Shoals in September 1780 were fiercely independent, but the threat to their way of life, and their very existence, made coming together a necessity.

Sevier and Shelby each brought around 240 men, from Washington and Sullivan Counties of North Carolina, respectively. William Campbell brought 400 Virginians, while McDowell brought 160 from Burke and Rutherford Counties in North Carolina.

These numbers would be built upon during the march in search of Ferguson. Benjamin Cleveland and Joseph Winston joined with 350 men from Wilkes and Surry Counties in North Carolina, while 400 men joined from South Carolina. It is worth noting that whatever the Overmountain Men were known as at the time, they were a minority in the small army.

Most estimates agree that around 1,100 of these men would engage Ferguson during the battle, giving the two sides roughly equal numbers.

Depiction of a "Virginia Mountaineer." (The Granger Collection/Alamy)

ORDER OF BATTLE

LOYALIST FORCES
Commanding Officer
Maj. Patrick Ferguson

Provincials
(Approximate strength 118, including officers)
American Volunteers
Maj. Patrick Ferguson
Adj. (Lt.) Anthony Allaire
King's American Regiment Detachment
Capt. Abraham DePeyster
Other officers
Adj. Daniel Blue
Ensign John Crookshank
Privates and NCOs   19
New Jersey Volunteers Regiment Detachment
Company commanders
Capt. Patrick Campbell
Capt. Joseph Crowell
Capt. Samuel Ryerson
Capt. John Taylor
Other officers
Lt. Martin Ryerson
Lt. William Stevenson
Privates and NCOs   52
Loyal American Regiment Detachment
Other officers
Lt. Duncan Fletcher
Privates and NCOs   17
Prince of Wales American Regiment Detachment
Privates and NCOs   17
King's Carolina Rangers Regiment Detachment
Other officers
Lt. Richard McGinnis

Loyalists
(Approximate strength 745, including officers)
Old Tryon County Regiment of Loyalist Militia (NC)
Col. Ambrose Mills
Maj. William Mills
Company commanders
Capt. Jonas Bradford
Capt. Willian Green
Privates and NCOs   2
Burke County Regiment of Loyalist Militia (NC)
Col. Vezey Husbands
Privates and NCOs   8
Rutherford County Regiment of Loyalist Militia (NC)
Company commanders
Capt. Aaron Bickerstaff
Capt. James Chitwood
Capt. Walter Gilkey
Capt. Grimes
Other officers
Lt. John Bibby
Lt. Lafferty
Privates and NCOs   1
Fair Forest Regiment of Loyalist Militia (SC)
Maj. Daniel Plummer
Maj. Jonathan Frost
Company commanders
Capt. William Bogin
Capt. James Campbell
Capt. Philip Coleman
Capt. William Gist
Capt. Shadrack Lantrey
Capt. William Lee
Capt. Elisha Robinson
Capt. James Shearer
Capt. James Vernon
Capt. Robert Whitley
Capt. Robert Wilson
Other officers
Lt. Alexander Chesney
Lt. James Brown
Lt. James Dickson
Lt. William Elliott
Ensign Hugh Grindle
Ensign John Beaver
Privates and NCOs   147
Spartan Regiment of Loyalist Militia (SC) Detachment
Company commanders
Capt. John Anderson
Capt. William Duman
Capt. William Duncan
Capt. James Gibbs
Capt. Isaac Gray
Capt. Nicholas Hawley
Capt. Patrick Moore
Capt. James Robins
Capt. Benjamin Wofford
Capt. William Young
Lt. Richard Mays
Other officers
Lt. John Ford, Jr.
Lt. Alven Hendrick
Lt. Samuel Young
Ensign James Hall
Privates and NCOs   126
Little River Regiment of Loyalist Militia
Maj. Patrick Cunningham
Company commanders
Capt. Andrew Cunningham
Capt. William Cunningham
Capt. John Dalrymple
Capt. William Helms
Capt. William Hendricks
Capt. Christopher Neeley
Capt. William Payne
Capt. Joseph Person
Other officers
Lt. Samuel Dalrymple
Lt. Thomas Johnson
Lt. Joseph Ray
Ensign John Hood
Ensign John Hunter
Ensign Henry Crum
Privates and NCOs   243
Long Cane Regiment of Loyalist Militia (SC) Detachment
Company commanders
Capt. David Larimore
Capt. George Long
Privates and NCOs   3
Steven's Creek Regiment of Loyalist Militia (SC)
Company commanders
Capt. Robert Anderson
Capt. Bailey Cheney
Capt. John Cotton

Capt. William Kirkland
Capt. Denas Nowland
Capt. Henry Rudolph
Capt. Thomas Whitehead
Capt. Hezekiah Williams
Other officers
Lt. Rowland Williams
Ensign Adam Fralick
Privates and NCOs   105
Dutch Fork Regiment of Loyalist Militia (SC) Detachment
Company commanders
Capt. William Ballentine
Capt. David Reese
Capt. Humphrey Williamson
Other officers
Lt. Thomas Bee
Lt. James Wilkinson
Privates and NCOs   6

Known Loyalist militiamen at Kings Mountain with no known company

South Carolina
Lt. Absolum Aughtey
Privates and NCOs   24
North Carolina
Privates and NCOs   14
Virginia
Privates and NCOs   1

Total of known* participants: 876

PATRIOT FORCES

(Note: This is an estimate of the men who fought in the actual battle. Sources vary widely on the numbers and composition of the Patriot militia.)
Commanding Officer
Col. William Campbell

Virginia Militia

(Approximate strength 153, including officers)
Col. Arthur Campbell
Augusta County Regiment
Company commanders
Capt. Samuel McCutcheon
Montgomery County Regiment
Company commanders
Capt. James Montgomery
Privates and NCOs   1
Rockbridge Rifles
Col. William Bowyer
Washington County Regiment
Col. William Campbell
Maj. William Edmonson
Adj. John Reid
Company commanders
Capt. David Beattie
Capt. Reese Bowen
Capt. David Campbell
Capt. John Campbell
Capt. Andrew Colville
Capt. Robert Craig
Capt. William Dougherty
Capt. James Dysart
Capt. John Edmondson
Capt. Robert Edmondson, Sr.
Capt. William Edmondson (mounted company)

Capt. John Hays
Capt. Robert Kennedy
Capt. William Love
Capt. Samuel McCutcheon
Capt. James Montgomery
Capt. Joshua Nichols
Lt. Thomas McCullough
Lt. William Russell, Jr.
Other officers
Lt. William Bartlett
Lt. William Blackburn
Lt. Robert Campbell
Lt. Samuel Newell
Lt. Trimble
Lt. Joseph Black
Lt. Andrew Kincannon
Lt. Samuel Meek
Lt. Patrick Campbell
Lt. William Crabtree
Lt. John Carroll
Lt./Ensign William Willoughby
2nd Lt. William Davison
2nd Lt. James Corry
2nd Lt. Andrew Edmondson
2nd Lt./Ensign John Beatty
Ensign Nathanial Dryden
Ensign Andrew Goff
Ensign Henry Dickenson
Ensign Thomas Shote
Ensign Armstrong
Ensign Robert Campbell
Ensign James Phillips
Ensign James Houston
Ensign Charles Robertson
Privates and NCOs   102

North Carolina Militia

(Approximate strength 672, including officers)
Col. Benjamin Cleveland
Burke County Regiment
Maj. Joseph 'Quaker Meadows Joe' McDowell
Maj. George Wilfong
Company commanders
Capt. Robert Ballew
Capt. Jonathan Camp/Kemp
Capt. Alexander Erwin
Capt. Edmund Fear
Capt. John Harden/Hardin
Capt. Thomas Hemphill
Capt. John Holmes
Capt. Thomas Kennedy
Capt. Thomas Lytle
Capt. Joseph 'Pleasant Gardens Joe' McDowell
Capt. Samuel Miller
Capt. Robert Patton (light horse company)
Capt. Adam Reep
Capt. John Russell
Capt. John Sigman
Capt. Daniel Smith
Capt. John Sorrell
Capt. David Vance
Capt. Patrick Watson
Capt. Joseph White
Capt. Samuel Woods/Wood
Capt. Young
Other officers
Lt. Van Horn
Privates and NCOs   38

*These are numbers of people whom various historians are confident actually took part in the battle, there may well have been more in action on the day.

Caswell County Regiment Detachment
Company commanders
Capt. John Douglas (light horse company)
Capt. John McMullen (light horse company)
Other officers
Lt. Thomas Neely
Lt. David Mitchell
Ensign John Barnett
Ensign Robert Culbertson
Privates and NCOs   14
Chatham County Regiment Detachment
Company commanders
Capt. William Gholson
Capt. William Griffin
Capt. John Hudgins
Privates and NCOs   3
Granville County Regiment Detachment
Company commanders
Capt. William Bennett
Other officers
Lt. Samuel Gray
Privates and NCOs   1
Guilford County Regiment Detachment
Company commanders
Capt. Hugh Fabush
Privates and NCOs   1
Lincoln County Regiment
Lt. Col. Frederick Hambright
Maj. John Barber
Maj. William Chronicle
Maj. Joseph Dickson
Maj. Francis McCorkle
Adj. Andrew Floyd
Company commanders
Capt. William Armstrong
Capt. James Baird
Capt. John Baldridge (mounted rifle company)
Capt. Samuel Caldwell
Capt. John Carruth
Capt. John Philip Dellinger
Capt. Samuel Espey (ranger company)
Capt. John Hardin Hambright
Capt. Malcolm Henry (mounted rifle company)
Capt. James Johnson/Johnston
Capt. Thomas Lofton
Capt. Samuel Martin
Capt. Charles Mattocks
Capt. John Mattocks
Capt. John Moore
Capt. William Moore
Capt. William Sherrill
Capt. John Weir
Other officers
Lt. James Hill
Lt. Gideon Robertson
Lt. Thomas White
Ensign John Berry
Ensign John Hall
Privates and NCOs   113
Mecklenburg County Regiment Detachment
Company commanders
Capt. Conrad Hise (light horse company)
Capt. James Ligert/Tigert
Capt. Magrath
Capt. James Reese
Capt. Thomas Shelby
Capt. Zaccheus Wilson
Privates and NCOs   4
Rowan County Regiment
Lt. Col. Matthew Brandon

Lt. Col. John Hampton
Company commanders
Capt. John Brandon/Brannon
Capt. Thomas Cowan
Capt. John Dickey
Capt. James Houston
Capt. Peter Mull
Capt. Richard Simmons
Capt. Benjamin Smith
Privates and NCOs   5
Rutherford County Regiment
Col. Andrew Hampton
Maj. James Gray
Maj. James Porter
Maj. Robert Porter
Company commanders
Capt. Adam Hampton (light horse company)
Capt. Benjamin Harden/Hardin
Capt. George Ledbetter
Capt. John McClain
Capt. John McClure
Capt. James McElhaney
Capt. Ephraim McLean
Capt. James Miller (light horse company)
Capt. George Paris
Capt. William Porter
Capt. Thomas Price
Capt. Moses Shelby
Capt. Richard Singleton
Capt. James Withrow
Other officers
Lt. William Walker
Privates and NCOs   31
Sullivan County Regiment
Col. Isaac Shelby
Maj. Evan Shelby, Jr.
Company commanders
Capt. Thomas Caldwell
Capt. Moses Cavett
Capt. Gilbert Christian
Capt. James Duff
Capt. James Elliott
Capt. William Johnston
Capt. John/Jack Martin
Capt. George Maxwell
Capt. John Pemberton (mounted rifle company)
Capt. John Sawyer/Sawyers
Capt. George Taylor
Capt. Roger Topp (ranger company)
Capt. Thomas Wallace
Capt. David Webb
Capt. Jonathan Webb
Other officers
Ensign John Sharp
Privates and NCOs   45
Surry County Regiment
Maj. Joseph Winston
Maj. Micajah Lewis
Maj. Edward Lovell
Company Commanders
Capt. Joseph Cloud/Cloyd (light horse company)
Capt. James Giddings
Capt. William Thrift Hughlett
Capt./Lt. Samuel Johnson (light horse company)
Capt. Joel Lewis
Capt. William Terrell Lewis
Capt. Salathiel Martin
Capt. Sam McDowell
Capt. William Meredith
Capt. Harrison Murray

Capt. Joseph Phillips
Capt. James Shepherd (dragoon company)
Capt. Henry Smith
Capt. Minor Smith
Other officers
Lt. Richard Shipp
Lt. Benjamin Humphreys
Lt. Ezekiel Young
Lt. James Martin Lewis
Lt. Shadrack Thompson
Lt. Joseph Martin
Lt. Obediah Martin
Lt. Peter Helton
Lt. Richard Varnum/Vernon
Lt. Adam Binkley
Lt. Samuel Houston
Lt. Daniel Martin
Ensign John Cleveland
Ensign Christopher Kirby
Ensign Lawrence Angell
Ensign Oliver Charles
Privates and NCOs   55
Washington County Regiment
Lt. Col. John Sevier
Lt. Col. John Lewis
Lt. Col. Charles Robertson
Maj. Isaac Lane
Maj. Benjamin Sharp
Maj. Jonathan Tipton
Maj. Jesse Walton
Adj. David Hickey
Company commanders
Capt. Jesse Bean/Beene
Capt. William Bean
Capt. Jacob Brown
Capt. Joel Callahan
Capt. Benjamin Clark
Capt. William Cox
Capt. James Crabtree
Capt. Finley
Capt. Ning Hawkins
Capt. Joseph Lusk
Capt. Alexander Moore
Capt. George North
Capt. John Patterson
Capt. James Pearce
Capt. Thomas Preston
Capt. George Russell
Capt. Robert Sevier (light horse company)
Capt. Valentine Sevier, Jr.
Capt. James Stinson
Capt. Christopher Taylor
Capt. Waring
Capt. Samuel Wear/Ware/Weir
Capt. Samuel Williams
Capt. James Wilson
Capt. Elijah Witt
Capt. Young
Other officers
Lt. John Sevier, Jr.
Lt. Isaac Lane
Lt. William Robertson
Lt. Alexander Greer
Lt. Wood
Lt. Daniel Kennedy
Ensign Jacob Brown, Jr.
Ensign John Singleton
Ensign Peter McLane
Privates and NCOs   62
Wilkes County Regiment

Col. Benjamin Cleveland
Lt. Col. William Shepherd
Maj. Joseph Harden
Company Commanders
Capt. Richard Allen
Capt. Daniel Bailey
Capt. John Barton (light horse company)
Capt. Thomas Biecknell
Capt. John Brown (mounted rifle company)
Capt. John Cleveland
Capt. Robert Cleveland
Capt. Abraham DeMoss
Capt. Jesse Hardin Franklin
Capt. Charles Gordon, Sr.
Capt. Moses Guest (light horse company)
Capt. Benjamin Herndon
Capt. William Jackson
Capt. John Kees
Capt. William Lenoir
Capt. John Morgan
Capt. Bethuel Riggs
Capt. Thurman
Capt. Walton
Lt. Martin Gambill
Other officers
Lt. Thomas Biecknell
Lt. Benjamin Guess
Lt. Charles Gordon, Jr.
Lt. Richard Stonecypher
Lt. Garrett Smithey
Lt. Thomas Ferguson
Lt. Hawson
Lt. Bernard Owens
Ensign Thomas Barton
Ensign Benjamin Guest
Ensign John Houston
Privates and NCOs   71

South Carolina Militia

(Approximate strength 234, including officers)
Camden District Regiment Detachment
Company commanders
Capt. James Coiel
Capt. William Goodwyn
Capt. John Weathers
Privates and NCOs   1
Fairfield Regiment Detachment
Company commanders
Capt. Samuel Lacey
Capt. Edward Martin
Capt. John Turner
Privates and NCOs   3
Hill's Regiment Detachment
Lt. Col. James Hawthorn
Maj. Samuel Tate
Company commanders
Capt. Jacob Barnett
Capt. James Giles
Capt. John Hollis
Capt. John Kincaid
Capt. William McKenzie
Privates and NCOs   9
Little River District Regiment
Col. James Williams
Lt. Col. Joseph Hayes
Maj. George Anderson
Maj. John Moore
Maj. Samuel Hammond
Company commanders
Capt. Mordecai Clark

Capt. Samuel Culbertson
Capt. James Dillard
Capt. Thomas Duggin
Capt. Samuel Ewing
Capt. William Graham
Capt. Pendleton Isbell
Capt. John Jones
Capt. John Smith
Capt. Isaac White (light horse or range company)
Capt. Daniel Williams
Other officers
Lt. Smith
Privates and NCOs   29

Lower District Regiment Detachment
Company commanders
Capt. John Walters
Privates and NCOs   1

New Acquisition District Regiment
Col. Samuel Watson
Lt. Col. Andrew Love
Maj. John Wallace
Company commanders
Capt. John Cunningham (mounted rifle company)
Capt. Robert Hanna
Capt. John Hawthorn
Capt. John Henderson
Capt. Joseph Howe
Capt. James Meek
Capt. Joseph Smith
Other officers
Lt. Samuel Carson
Lt. Thomas Henderson
Lt. John Kincaid
Privates and NCOs   16

Roebuck's Battalion of Spartan Regiment
Col. Benjamin Roebuck
Company commanders
Capt. Andrew Barry
Capt. Ambrose Finnel
Capt. Vardry McBee
Capt. Parson
Capt. George Roebuck
Capt. James Smith
Capt. Robert Thomas
Capt. Moses Wood
Other officers
Lt. Josiah Tanner
Privates and NCOs   14

2nd Spartan Regiment/1st Spartan Regiment Detachment
Col. Thomas Brandon
Lt. Col. James Steen
Maj. John Moore
Maj. Thomas Young
Company commanders
Capt. John Boyer
Capt. Gabriel Brown
Capt. John Collins
Capt. Daniel Duff
Capt. William Grant
Capt. Benjamin Jolly (light horse company)
Capt. John McCool
Capt. John Putnam

Capt. William Smith
Capt. William Taylor
Capt. Moses White
Capt. William Young
Other officers
Lt. William Grant
Lt. William W. DeSaussure
Lt. William Giles
Lt. Joseph Hughes
Lt. Nathan Williford
Lt. Absalom Thompson
Lt. Benjamin Jones
Lt. James Martindale
Privates and NCOs   34

Turkey Creek Regiment
Col. Edward Lacey
Lt. Col. John Nixon
Maj. John Adair
Adj. John Miller
Company commanders
Capt. James Johnson
Capt. John Mills
Capt. John Moffett
Capt. James Ramsey
Capt. John Steel (light horse company)
Capt. James Styles
Capt. John Thompson
Other officers
Lt. Robert Walker
Lt. Josiah Tanner
Privates and NCOs   20

Upper Ninety Six District Regiment Detachment
Lt. Col. Robert Anderson
Maj. James McCall
Company commanders
Capt. John Irwin
Capt. Samuel Kerr
Capt. Thomas Winn
Privates and NCOs   9

Georgia Militia

(Approximate strength 15, including officers)
Clarke's Regiment Detachment
Maj. William Candler
Maj. John Cunningham
Company commanders
Capt. Patrick Carr
Capt. John Clark
Capt. Josiah Dunn
Capt. William Hammett
Capt. Richard Heard
Capt. Stephen Johnson
Privates and NCOs   7

Unknown Regiment
Lt. John Bird
Lt. Andrew Caruthers
Lt. Arthur Johnson
Lt. David Smith
Lt. Frederick Williams
Privates and NCOs   42

Total of known* participants: 1,116

*These are numbers of people whom various historians are confident actually took part in the battle, there may well have been more in action on the day.

OPPOSING PLANS

LOYALIST

Ferguson's corps operated as part of the wider plan Cornwallis had put into operation for the invasion of North Carolina. This invasion, despite the tenuous grip British forces had on South Carolina, was considered unavoidable by the British commander in the South, but there were signs of trouble from the start. Echoing the debacle at Moore's Creek in 1776, North Carolina Loyalists had again risen prematurely, and again been routed, this time at Ramsour's Mill on June 20, 1780. Cornwallis saw no hope for the colony unless a significant army of regulars appeared on the scene. To this end, he made a bold decision.

"I think," he wrote to Clinton in New York, 10 days after the defeat at Ramsour's Mill, "that with the force at present under my command... I can leave South Carolina in security and march about the beginning of September with a body of troops into the back part of North Carolina with the greatest probability of reducing that province to its duty."

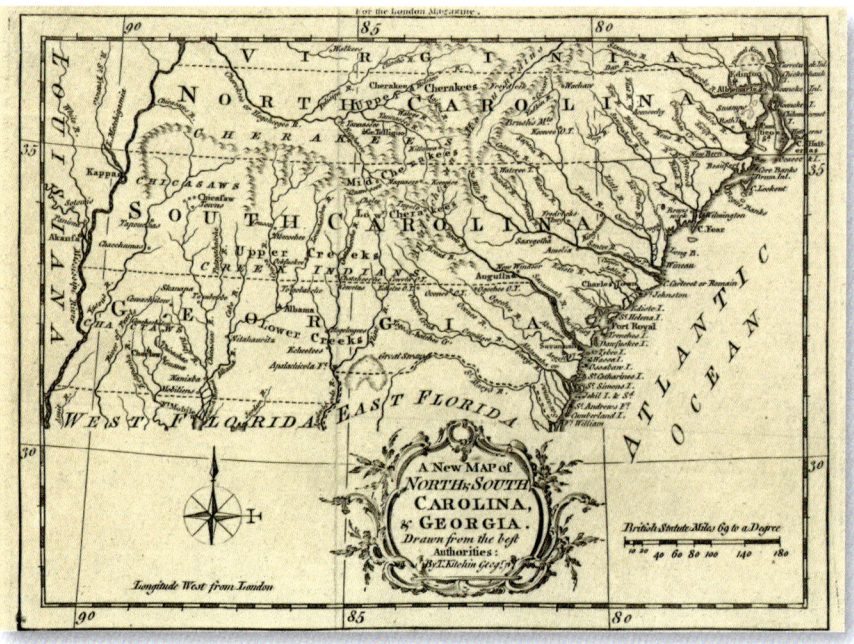

"A new map of North & South Carolina, & Georgia," by Thomas Kitchin, published in 1765, gives an impression of the vast area Britain was hoping to control with just a few thousand men. (Library of Congress, Geography and Map Division)

Furthermore, Cornwallis stated that he believed that once it had been returned to loyalty, the colony could be left for Loyalists to police, freeing the regular army for further operations elsewhere. It was an exact repeat of the planning for the invasion of South Carolina – but South Carolina was far from settled, and now Cornwallis was spreading his meager resources even more thinly. Perhaps, as a naturally aggressive officer, he could not see any other way of using the men under his command.

Ferguson's role in the forthcoming campaign was to be a hazardous one, and it is perhaps surprising that Cornwallis entrusted it to him, having displayed a somewhat lukewarm opinion of the man and of militia in general. Ferguson's job would be to screen the left flank of Cornwallis' army as it advanced into North Carolina. This would mean taking on the Patriot backcountry militia, who had proven to be rather more effective than their Loyalist counterparts. After entering Tryon County, Ferguson was to join the rest of the army in Charlotte in preparation for a further advance deeper into North Carolina.

Ferguson was most definitely not ordered to whip up a hornets' nest of opposition, but it has long been claimed that he did exactly this with an ill-judged threat to the territories over the mountains, although recent scholarship suggests this threat may have been exaggerated. Even so, Cornwallis' plan was risky from the start, and built upon weak foundations. The unreliability of his intelligence, for instance, was amply demonstrated by his belief that Charlotte would prove a suitable staging post for him to draw in Loyalist militia from the surrounding area. In contrast, once he arrived, he found Mecklenburg County to be "the most rebellious and inveterate that I have met with in this country, not excepting any part of the Jerseys." Not only was it an unsuitable place to attract Loyalists, it was doubtful whether he could even hold it without committing a considerable body of men to its defense. He was then faced with the choice of advancing further, with his line of communications with the main British base in Charleston already tenuous, or to withdraw and think again.

The decision would be made for him at Kings Mountain.

"The Smoky Mountains," as painted by Robert Hinshelwood. (The Print Collector/Heritage Images via Getty Images)

PATRIOT

There was little in the way of grand strategy in Patriot thinking in the run-up to Kings Mountain, but none was needed. Purely tactical operations were all that was required to confound British plans. So long as Patriot militia survived – a few hundred men here, a few hundred there – they could make Cornwallis' job an impossible one.

Although the British consistently viewed their operations as a liberation, to at least half the population it was an occupation, with all the attendant difficulties. The Americans would continue to rebuild their regular armies to face the British in set-piece battles, but the real damage was being done by small bodies of Patriots against similarly small bodies of regulars, provincial troops, and Loyalist militia.

The threat posed by Ferguson, however, was on a different scale. With 1,000 or so militia under his command it would take a substantial force to tackle him. Gathering enough men for the task was only part of the process – giving them effective command would also be important, and the independent nature of the men in question made that a tricky proposition. In truth, no commander would wield much influence outside of his own local militia group, so the small army would hold together only as long as everyone agreed with the chosen course of action.

The basic aim was to destroy Ferguson's command, and ideally to kill or capture Ferguson himself. This was not an attempt to deter or warn off – the Overmountain Men had been stirred and would not want to have to face a similar threat another few weeks or months down the line. That is not to say there was no thought of failure. If they could not find Ferguson and destroy his command, they would unite with any other bands of Patriot militia they ran into and fight whatever enemy forces were in the area – but this would be a raid of limited duration, and the ultimate success would rely in large part on Ferguson's willingness to stand his ground. If he kept moving, or if he linked up with the main army under Cornwallis, he would be out of reach.

This rifle dates to around 1760 and features an octagonal barrel with seven grooves. The buttplate is engraved with the initials "SH." (© Royal Armouries)

THE CAMPAIGN

The initial British move into the South Carolina backcountry went well. An arc of forward bases was being established, built around the anchor points of Augusta and Ninety Six. Plans were being shaped for the capture of Camden as well, and a string of small-scale victories suggested that everything was going according to plan.

Banastre Tarleton in particular was proving to be a major problem for the Patriots. Victories at Monck's Corner (April 14), Lenud's Ferry (May 6), and Waxhaws (May 29) kept British spirits high and seemed to signal the collapse of organized resistance in the area. This proved to be wishful thinking. The Patriots kept coming, and inevitably some of the clashes with British forces began to go their way.

On July 12, Patriot militia defeated a British force that included trained provincials and even a few members of the famous British Legion (although Tarleton was not present). The Battle of Williamson's Plantation (often referred to as "Huck's Defeat") saw Captain Christian Huck's Loyalist force completely destroyed by Patriots under Colonel William Bratton. More than a hundred Loyalists were killed, wounded, or captured, while the Patriots had just one killed, one wounded, and one captured. Only 24 of the British force escaped and Huck himself was among the dead.

On July 30, Patriots under Isaac Shelby captured Thicketty Fort (the British commander, Captain Patrick Moore, was reprimanded for surrendering without a fight). On the same day, Colonel Thomas Sumter led a determined attack on Rocky Mount, a fortified British position overlooking the Catawba River. This was a bold move – three of the buildings at the post had been prepared for defense by the cutting of loopholes, and they were further protected by a ditch and abatis. A spy informed Sumter that there were around 300 Loyalist militia and provincials in the fort.

Attacking the position, Sumter's men assumed that the main building, with its thin clapboard walls, would make for easy pickings, but the Loyalists had been at work, placing logs a foot away from the inside of

Tarleton's slaughter of Buford's command at Waxhaws led to the emergence of a new battle cry for the Patriots – "Tarleton's quarter" would henceforth be a call for no mercy. (Prints, Drawings and Watercolors from the Anne S. K. Brown Military Collection, Brown Digital Repository, Brown University Library)

Events in the South before Kings Mountain, 1780

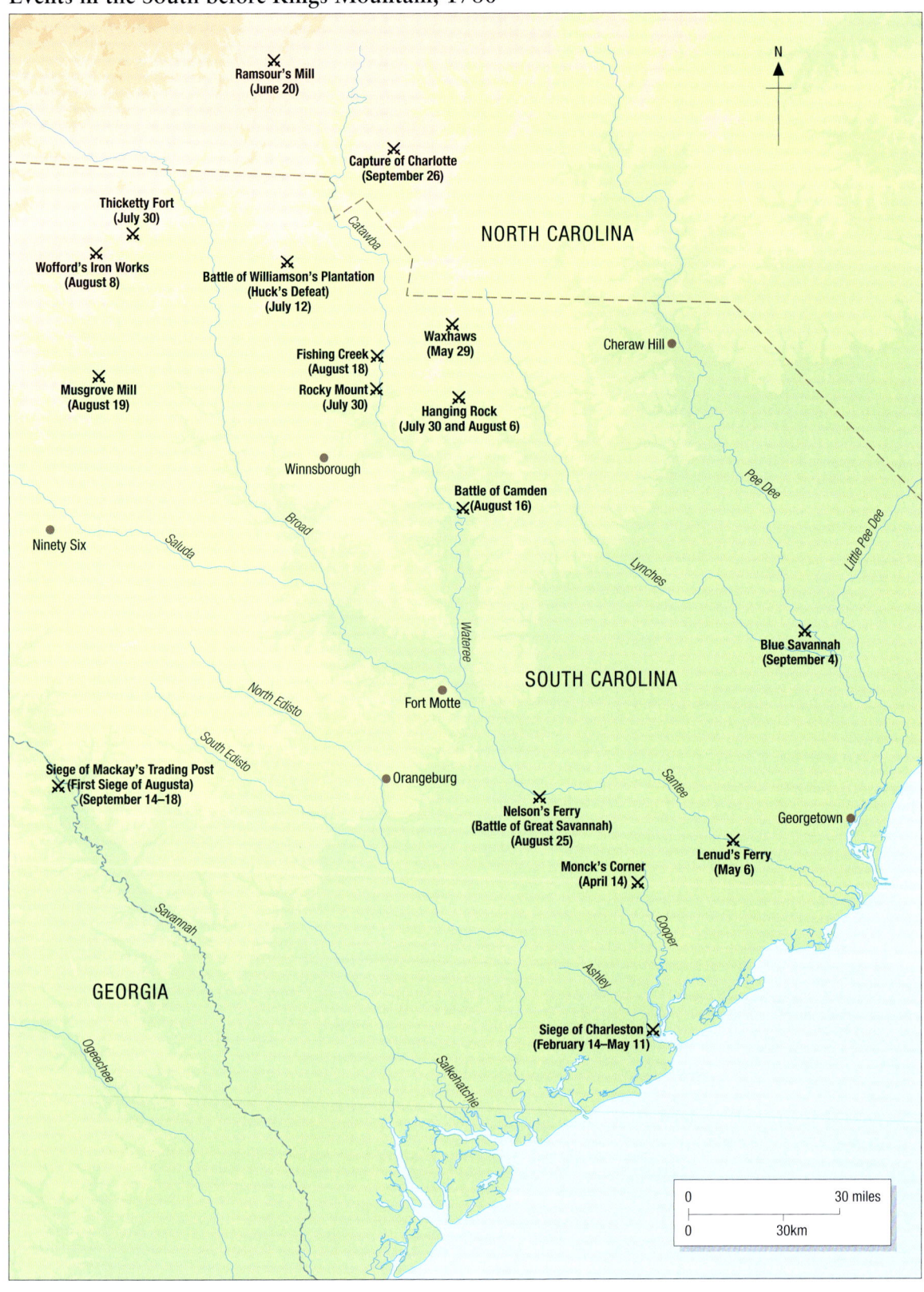

Visitors to Philadelphia's Museum of the American Revolution can get a taste of how it felt to be charged by Tarleton's Legion. (Randy Duchaine/Alamy)

the walls and filling the cavity with clay, rendering the lower portion of the building entirely bulletproof. After eight hours of fighting, in which Sumter attempted to get men close enough to the fortified buildings to set them alight, the attack was called off. The British forces had prevailed, but the determination of the attack was illuminating.

Also on July 30, a skirmish at Hanging Rock saw Patriots under Major William Davie capture 60 horses and 100 muskets after a surprise attack against a much larger garrison. A week later, Sumter and Davie joined forces for a more concerted attack on Hanging Rock, which resulted in significant losses to the British garrison (25 dead, 175 wounded, and 73 captured).

Portrait of Thomas Sumter. (From *The American Generals, from the Founding of the Republic to the Present Time* by John Frost)

South Carolina was clearly far from pacified, but Ferguson was making steady progress in recruiting Loyalists. The Inspector of Militia had been enjoying success in the district around Ninety Six, forming 1,800 Loyalists into six regiments – the Long Cane Regiment (Colonel Richard King), the Steven's Creek Regiment (Colonel John Cotton), the Spartan Regiment (sometimes called the Upper Regiment, under Colonel Zacharias Gibbs), the Dutch Fork Regiment (Colonel Daniel Clary), and Moses Kirkland's Regiment.

While Ferguson gathered and trained his men, trouble was on the way from a new source. In Georgia, Lieutenant Colonel Thomas Brown had hanged five Patriots back on June 5.

Sumter's exploits at Hanging Rock were dramatized in a popular magazine in 1904. (*The Boys of "76"* magazine by Harry Moore, Digital Library at Villanova University)

Victory at the Battle of Camden again created the illusion that Britain was in control of events in the South, but partisan activity remained a major headache. (Prints, Drawings and Watercolors from the Anne S. K. Brown Military Collection, Brown Digital Repository, Brown University Library)

This was not unprecedented, as both sides would occasionally hang men who had broken parole or switched sides in the conflict, but the harsh action convinced many who had given their parole to the British to take up arms again. One of these men was Colonel Elijah Clarke, who began gathering a Patriot force in the Ninety Six neighborhood.

That force soon numbered around 1,000, 600 of which were under Clarke when he ambushed a small number of Ferguson's men (14 American Volunteers and 130 militia) at Wofford's Iron Works on August 8. The Loyalists were driven off with somewhere between eight and 34 casualties (accounts vary), leaving behind as many as 50 prisoners.

Clarke had been wounded and even briefly captured during the melee, but he was able to claim a victory and would have more contributions to make in the run-up to Kings Mountain.

THE DESTRUCTION OF GATES' GRAND ARMY

The Battle of Camden was exactly what the British needed at this point. As the militia war ebbed and flowed, but crucially showed no signs of burning itself out, a conventional pitched battle was just the kind of thing to restore confidence and a sense of control. General Horatio Gates offered his army on a platter on August 16, and Cornwallis wasted no time in carving it up, delivering a crushing defeat that again seemed to open up the entire colony.

Once more, the Patriot militia were alone in the South. As always happened, the Americans would put together another army, but for now it was small bands of partisans that would continue the struggle. Sumter was in command of the largest such band still operating in South Carolina, and was therefore targeted by Cornwallis, who unleashed his most potent attacking unit, Banastre Tarleton's British Legion. In much the same way that Tarleton had followed up Charleston with a devastating blow at

Waxhaws, he now followed up Camden by destroying Sumter's command at Fishing Creek.

Sumter had made a nuisance of himself by capturing supplies that were on their way to Cornwallis' army. He would have sent the supplies on to Gates as he approached with his army, but the route taken by the American general was unknown to Sumter, so he kept 50 supply wagons with his command, which inevitably slowed him down. After Gates' defeat, Sumter was withdrawing towards Charlotte when Tarleton was set on his trail.

From Cornwallis' correspondence with Clinton in New York and Lord George Germain (the American Secretary) in London, it was clear how important Sumter's command was considered to be. It might, Cornwallis mentioned to Germain on August 21, "prove a foundation for assembling the routed army." Therefore, he "despatched Lt Colonel Tarleton with the Legion cavalry and infantry and the corps of light infantry, making in all about 350 men, with orders to attack him wherever he could find him."

Bearing in mind that Sumter was believed to have around 1,000 men with him, it is clear how highly Cornwallis thought of Tarleton – his orders gave no room for demurring. At the same time, units under Ferguson and Lieutenant Colonel George Turnbull were ordered to cut off any line of retreat for Sumter, but in the event they were not needed.

Sumter knew he was a hunted man, but he was not aware that Tarleton was tracking him. If he had been, he would undoubtedly have moved more quickly, which would probably have involved ditching the 50 wagons of supplies, 300 head of cattle, and 250 prisoners that his exploits had netted him. He had 100 Continentals from the 5th Maryland Regiment with him, along with 300 from his own Brigade of Partisans, 300 men of the Wilkes County Militia under Lieutenant Colonel Elijah Isaacs, and a pair of brass three-pounders.

By August 17, Tarleton was looking at Sumter's campfires from the opposite side of the Catawba. What happened next is difficult to explain. Sumter was alerted to Tarleton's presence and broke camp, but he only marched eight miles before stopping at midday, at Fishing Creek. He must have been aware of the reputation of Tarleton, which involved not only lightning-quick movement, but also instant and uncompromising attack once his

Although the Continental Army elements in Gates' army performed well at the Battle of Camden, they were let down by the Patriot militia. (Library of Congress)

Lieutenant Colonel George Turnbull had left the Army and was settled in New York when war broke out. He was then commissioned in the New York Volunteers, which became the 3rd American Regiment. (CC-BY-SA 4.0 via Wikimedia Commons)

The "Cornwallis House" became the British headquarters in Camden after the rout of General Gates' army. (From *Historic Camden, Part One* by Thomas J. Kirkland and Robert M. Kennedy)

Banastre Tarleton was the highly aggressive commander of the British Legion, a combined force of infantry and dragoons that earned a fearsome reputation in the South. (Prints, Drawings and Watercolors from the Anne S. K. Brown Military Collection, Brown Digital Repository, Brown University Library)

enemy had been found. Sure enough, Tarleton crossed the river, selected 60 of his infantry to "double-up" on the dragoon mounts, and urged his reduced command on at high speed. Legend has it that two women, who had passed through Sumter's camp, gave Tarleton detailed intelligence. His force now comprised 40 light infantrymen from the 71st, 100 British Legion dragoons, and 20 British Legion infantry. With these men he had no hesitation in attacking more than 700 soldiers under Sumter.

Not many men could take a siesta while Tarleton was on their heels, but Sumter was dozing under a wagon (perhaps convinced that he had a strong defensive position, with ravines protecting both of his flanks) when the British arrived. One of Sumter's officers would later comment that "the men were very hungry, had marched for three days, very hot weather and very weary," so it is possible he could not push them any harder. Whatever the reasoning, the Americans' situation was about to get a lot worse.

Cornwallis' verdict of the ensuing battle was succinct: "Lt Colonel Tarleton executed this service with his usual activity and military address." There were certainly all the hallmarks of a Tarleton battle. After finding his quarry, he lost no time, lining his men up and sounding the charge. A chaotic scene unfolded, as some of the Patriots were scattered. The Maryland Continentals tried to get to where their muskets were stacked, and some men, who had been bathing in the river, tried to escape. A couple of pockets of resistance formed, but the general scene was one of chaos and the usual tales regarding

Tarleton's actions – there were reports that promises were made that men who surrendered would be treated well, only for them to be cut down when they gave themselves up. How much of this is true is uncertain, but it was a familiar refrain from the Patriots when "Bloody Ban" was at work.

Sumter himself escaped, although in undignified and almost comical circumstances. Roused from his nap, he mounted a horse with neither boots nor hat, called to his men to make their escape as best they could, and then galloped away before knocking himself unconscious on a low branch. After coming to, he was able to remount his horse and escape.

More than half of his command were not so lucky. A total of 50 men were killed and another 100 wounded, while 310 were captured. All of the Marylanders were among the captives, and Tarleton also liberated the 250 prisoners Sumter had been guarding, as well as recapturing the wagons and beef cattle. A thousand Patriot muskets fell into his hands, as well as the three-pounder cannons, which had been able to fire just one shot between them during the entire battle.

The next day, the remains of Sumter's command returned to the battlefield to bury their dead, tend to their wounded, and attempt to digest what had happened. Cornwallis had no doubts over how important the victory was. "This action is too brilliant to need any comment of mine," he wrote to Germain. "The rebel forces being at present dispersed, the internal commotions and insurrections in the province will now subside, but I shall give directions to inflict exemplary punishment on some of the most guilty in hopes to deter others in future from sporting with allegiance, with oaths, and with the lenity and generosity of the British Government."

Cornwallis was promising to take a harder line with the Patriots, but as he was writing to Germain, his comments on the state of the province had already proved out of touch. On the day after Sumter's command was badly mauled at Fishing Creek, another "internal commotion" broke out, at Musgrove Mill, and this commotion had a very different outcome.

Following the capture of Thicketty Fort, Ferguson had been next to draw the attention of the Patriots under Shelby and Clarke (Shelby was eager to do more with his men before their enlistments ran out). Believing there to be around 200 Loyalists in a detached camp, away from the main body of Ferguson's corps, a raid was planned to surprise them.

Site of the Battle of Musgrove Mill, where the Patriot position atop a ridge fended off a British attack. (John Foxe, public domain, via Wikimedia Commons)

Shelby and Clarke set off with an indeterminate number of men (Shelby claimed the total number of Patriot militia to be as high as 700) and they were soon joined by Colonel James Williams. It is not clear how many men faced them, but it was more than they had bargained for because more Loyalists and a unit of provincials had joined the British camp. Shelby reckoned the enemy numbered around 700, while Williams offered a lower estimate, believing there to have been 500.

By the time this was realized, there was no hope of an easy withdrawal. The Patriots had ridden their horses hard, covering 40 miles in a single night, and they needed rest.

As well as this, the Loyalists had been alerted to their presence. One of their patrols had stumbled across a Patriot scouting party and, after shots were exchanged, several of them had ridden off to warn their comrades. Escape was now impossible.

Hastily constructing a defensive barricade from felled trees (it reportedly reached chest height in just half an hour), the Patriots set up a strong position. No single man took control of the entire force – each section took orders from its own commanding officer. On the right flank, Shelby positioned his 300 men. Williams' South Carolinians, 200-strong, occupied the center of the line, while an unknown number of Clarke's Georgia militia held the left flank, with 40 more acting as a reserve behind the line. Two parties of 20 mounted men further secured each flank and were kept hidden as much as possible.

The Loyalists held a conference after their returning patrolmen warned them of the enemy force in the vicinity. Lieutenant Colonel Alexander Innes was in command and was apparently in a hurry, because he ignored the advice to wait for a party of 100 mounted Loyalists, who would be returning to the camp soon. He quickly organized his men into three columns and marched out.

The 200 provincials with Innes were from the South Carolina Royalists, the light company of the 3rd Battalion New Jersey Volunteers, and the 1st Battalion of Delancey's Brigade, while the Loyalists (between 100 and 300 strong) were from the Ninety Six District Brigade.

The Loyalists were provoked into a reckless approach by Captain Shadrack Inman, who led a party of 25 mounted riflemen to goad them. He repeatedly approached the marching Loyalists and fell back, until they came within range of the defensive works.

The Loyalists apparently fired first, after dismounting, but they were at too great a range to do any damage. They then charged forward with bayonets levelled. Bayonets held a special horror for the Patriot militia, who did not use them, but with the added security of the breastworks they stood their ground, exhorted by their officers to hold their fire until they could either see the whites of their enemies' eyes or the buttons on their uniforms, depending on which version you believe.

When the Patriots did open fire, it was an effective volley, checking the Loyalists, who bravely returned to the attack. It seems to have taken a while for the column of provincials to reach the battle, but when they also attacked with bayonets, Shelby's men were driven back until Clarke's reserve troops steadied the position once more.

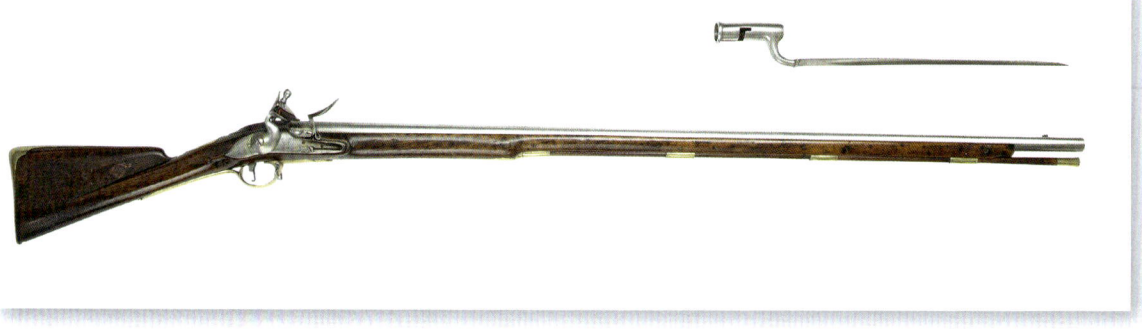

A Long Land Service Pattern 1742 musket and bayonet, of the kind issued to Loyalist units during the revolution. (© Royal Armouries)

The high-pitched "Indian-style" war cries of the Patriots added a nightmarish element to a battle that was extremely one sided. First the Loyalists broke, then the provincials, and then the Patriots pursued them for some distance. Captain DePeyster, present among the Loyalist force, would later recognize the battle cries he heard from Shelby's men on Kings Mountain, referring to them as "the damned yelling boys."

An estimated 63 of the British force were killed, 90 wounded and 70 taken prisoner. It was a devastating toll, especially when compared to just 12 casualties on the Patriot side. Innes may have regretted not waiting for his extra 100 men to return from patrol and he paid a stiff price for his impetuousness, taking severe wounds to his neck and thigh during the fighting.

Fired up by his success, Shelby was of a mind to continue, and the British post of Ninety Six was a tempting target. Referred to by some as the "Gibraltar of South Carolina," it was a symbol of continued British presence and a beacon to potential Loyalists. It was therefore a prime target, but devastating news was about to arrive. A messenger from Charles McDowell informed Shelby of the defeat of Gates at Camden. The British no longer needed to be wary of a sizeable regular army in their territory, and that meant they could hunt down the militia bands. With Ferguson close by, there was no doubting the danger now faced by Shelby's men. Accordingly, they began the long journey back over the mountains. In two days they covered 100 miles, riding to the point of exhaustion, but not daring to move more slowly.

Ferguson was indeed in pursuit. At 2200hrs on the evening of August 19, he was setting off to relieve Innes and prevent the Patriots from moving against Ninety Six, but this move was soon countermanded. Cornwallis called Ferguson to him at Camden, where he would be informed of his role in the forthcoming invasion of North Carolina.

For now, the Overmountain Men had returned to their homes, but it was to prove a brief interlude. They would soon be crossing the mountains again, with deadly effect.

CORNWALLIS' OFFENSIVE

Cornwallis had no choice but to rely heavily on Loyalist militia in his planning – he simply did not have sufficient men to do without them. Among his many biographers, Franklin and Mary Wickwire were especially pithy in their assessment of the militia, noting that "loyalist leaders recruited unwisely, rose inopportunely, and acted indecisively."

Still, the move into North Carolina appeared both natural and essential to Cornwallis, despite the fact that the performance of Loyalists there had done little to inspire confidence. After the routing of Gates at Camden, Cornwallis had "dispatched proper people into North Carolina to exhort our friends in that province to take arms, to seize military stores and magazines of the enemy, and to intercept all straglers [sic] of the routed army." The Loyalists had been hapless enough to dither over their responsibilities, allowing Gates himself to travel through Hillsborough with a guard of just six men.

Despite this, as Cornwallis informed Germain, "They continue, however, to give me the strongest assurances of support when His Majesty's troops shall have penetrated into the interior parts of the province." It was a familiar refrain, but, like a favorite fairy tale, the British never tired of hearing it.

Ferguson was aware of the sideways glances his men were attracting, largely due to the failure of other Loyalist leaders. On August 29, he wrote to Cornwallis, referring to a conversation between the two of them during their conference. Ferguson, who had spoken in favor of his men, clearly did not feel he had made his point effectively, and begged the indulgence of his commanding officer as he set out his case more carefully in writing. He pointed out that many of the Loyalist units that had performed badly throughout the region had been brought together in a haphazard fashion, without the benefit of sufficient training from British officers. Recruiting had been so slapdash that many Patriots had been allowed into the ranks of Loyalist units, with disastrous results.

In contrast, Ferguson pointed out that "the militia of 96 that have been admitted to bear arms are certainly loyal, almost to a man. They have been some time under discipline, by their own regulations have given proof that they are convinced of the necessity of order and obedience to their own safety and success, and taken measures to make it the interest of every man to do his duty."

In short, Ferguson's Loyalists were superior to anybody else's, and he was confident that they would remain steady even when far from their own homes – this of course was an essential quality as the British prepared to move into North Carolina. Ferguson did admit that in general Loyalists were less "warlike" than their Patriot counterparts, but he believed that "those that accompany our victorious army will soon be inspired with some of its confidence, and those who are detach'd upon offensive service, if fairly pitted, will also gain confidence."

Ferguson went further, suggesting that a second corps of Loyalists, in addition to his own and of equal size, would further protect the flank of the main army. Two such bodies, each numbering 1,000 men, would be able to join the main army within 12 hours or keep its flank clear of enemy activity. He made another admission at the end of his letter, stating that he could not be sure how his men would fair in "firm action," but that he had no doubts they could perform valuable service in the pursuit of a defeated foe.

It was not a ringing endorsement of the men under his command, but it was a fair one, and it would have given Cornwallis pause for thought. His plan put a huge responsibility on Ferguson's men – they would be screening his flank, clearing the territory of Patriot militia and then joining up with them for offensive operations once in North Carolina. Cornwallis had gone on the record in a letter to Clinton, admitting that "it may be doubted by some whether the invasion of North Carolina may be a prudent measure, but I am convinced it is a necessary one." Clearly, he realized his decision was something of a gamble, and this is reinforced when considering another letter to the commander-in-chief, which revealed a shocking lack of faith in Ferguson's men.

"Ferguson is to move into Tryon County with some militia," Cornwallis wrote on August 29, "whom he says he is sure he can depend upon for doing their duty and fighting well; but I am sorry to say that his own experience, as well as that of every other officer, is totally against him."

Clinton, who would spend the bulk of his life after the war nurturing grievances and writing his own account of the conflict, was therefore justified in mentioning, in that account, how starkly Cornwallis' orders contradicted his opinions. "We shall consequently be naturally surprised," Clinton noted, "to find His Lordship [Cornwallis], notwithstanding the decided opinions he had just given to the Minister and me on the subject, immediately detaching Major Ferguson with this very corps into Tryon County, to the west of the Catawba at a very considerable distance from his army."

It is interesting to note that Ferguson had his own ideas on how South Carolina might be controlled. He suggested the building of blockhouses, capable of holding 60 men and two guns, "to command at once all the Principal avenues & means of transportation by Land & water where they cross each other." This was not a particularly insightful concept – it would have been an immense undertaking, and such outposts would have been easy prey for a Patriot force of any size.

In late August, Cornwallis was chafing at his inability to start operations. His army was not only recovering from the Battle of Camden, it was also ravaged by illness. The 71st Regiment in particular had been rendered completely ineffective by sickness, and he faced the prospect of having to start his campaign in two stages. The first, which he hoped to launch around September 8, would see a first column move to Charlotte and Salisbury to set up a base. The second wave would then follow around 10 days later, bringing supplies and convalescents. Moving men who were in the early stages of recovery was a risk, but Cornwallis pointed out that even a march of just 40 or 50 miles would bring them into a healthier part of the country. Such were the myriad factors to be weighed up by the British commander in the South. Perhaps, with so much on his mind, he had been forced to simply hope that Ferguson would fulfill his role in the forthcoming campaign.

Minor flare-ups and skirmishes continued in the South as Cornwallis put his plan into motion. At Nelson's Ferry, on August 25, men from the 63rd Regiment and the Prince of Wales American Regiment were attacked by Francis Marion. The small British force, numbering just 36, had been guarding 150 Continental Army prisoners taken at Camden. Marion's men killed or captured 24 of the guards and freed 147 of the prisoners – but the Continentals, from Maryland and Delaware, had seen enough of the war. Many refused point blank to go with Marion and insisted on marching back into captivity at Charleston, while most of the rest quietly slipped away over the following days. Only three stayed with the partisan leader.

Spurred into a response, the British sent Major James Wemyss and 300 men to track Marion down. Marion set a small ambush for the British column, in which losses were equal (about 30 on each side). Reinforced by 400 more men, Wemyss pressed on, but Marion, living up to his nickname of "the Swamp Fox," was able to elude the larger force. It was symptomatic of the problems of partisan warfare – the British needed to commit men in large numbers to be sure of their own safety and Marion's 60 men had temporarily occupied 700 British.

An idealized depiction of Francis Marion riding through woodland, from an original painting by Alonzo Chappel. (Archive Photos/Getty Images)

"A British wagon-train surprised by Marion." (From *The Story of the Revolution* by Henry Cabot Lodge via Library of Congress)

On September 4, Marion added still further to his growing reputation at Blue Savannah, tackling a larger force of Loyalists under Major Micajah Ganey, formerly an officer under Marion. Although facing around 250 men, Marion set another ambush and killed or wounded 30 of Ganey's force at the cost of just four men wounded.

As well as these outbursts of violence in South Carolina, which put into question Cornwallis' intention of vacating the colony, an action on a far larger scale was about to take place in Georgia, and its repercussions would directly influence events in the build-up to Kings Mountain.

THE SIEGE OF MACKAY'S TRADING POST

When Shelby took his Overmountain Men back to their homes following the fall of Camden, Clarke returned to Georgia and began gathering men for partisan action there. Georgia had been mostly quiet since the capture of Savannah in December 1778. An expedition to capture Augusta had been planned, with 1,400 men under the command of Brigadier General James Paterson earmarked for the job, but that had been shelved when Clinton called on Paterson's men to help with the reduction of Charleston. Augusta had therefore remained in rebel hands, with the Loyalist commander Thomas Brown left at Savannah with his King's Rangers, ready to march on the town when ordered.

The subsequent fall of Charleston had dampened Patriot spirits as well as lifting those of the Loyalists. In this new mood of optimism, Alexander Innes claimed that a force of just 300 men could walk into Augusta and then on into the Georgia backcountry unopposed. Taking this opinion on board, Clinton ordered Brown to advance with the 300 men under his command. Most of these were Brown's own King's Rangers, but he also had some Georgia Loyalists and a handful of provincial soldiers from other units under his command.

Patriots from the South Carolina and Georgia militias had been occupying Augusta, but the South Carolinians departed after the fall of Charleston and only 50 of the Georgians remained. On June 8, Innes was proved correct – the small garrison melted away before the advance of Brown's men, and Augusta was under British control. The effect was profound. Georgia appeared to have been completely pacified as residents of Augusta and the backcountry sent petitions to the governor, Sir James Wright, to restore royal rule over the colony.

The occupation of Augusta also allowed the British to re-establish relations with their old allies, the Creek and Cherokee. Brown held the office of Superintendent of Indian Affairs in the region, and there was a lot of work to be done. Squatting on Native land had become rife and in the absence of British authority nothing had been done to curtail it, leading to dissatisfaction and even hostility on the part of the former allies. Brown sent men to dismantle Fort Rutledge, which had been illegally constructed on Native land, and ordered the removal of the squatters. Relations with the Creek and Cherokee began to improve immediately.

Despite the apparent lack of urgency regarding Augusta, it was of vital strategic importance to the British. As well as strengthening relations with their Native allies and securing the western flank of their line of posts, it was situated on the Savannah River, making it the most obvious route to get supplies to Ninety Six. Brown understood this and asked for permission to put the small

Sir Alexander Cuming meeting the Cherokee in 1730. After his visit, he returned to London with seven Cherokee chiefs and an "Agreement of Peace and Friendship" was signed between the two nations. (The Print Collector/Heritage Images/Alamy)

town into a more defensible state. An old stockade, Fort Augusta, was the only fortified building in the town, and it had been constructed in 1737. Its wooden walls were outdated and badly deteriorating. Brown asked for authorization to construct new defensive works and was supported in this by Balfour at Ninety Six.

By now, Cornwallis was in command in the South and his reply was surprising. He forbade the construction of anything except field works, and although he did not explain his thinking to Brown, it is clear that the expense of more substantial buildings was his primary objection. In a letter to the governor, he demonstrated how much this was playing on his mind, dismissing a request for more troops by saying, "so long as we are in Possession of the whole Power and Force of South Carolina, the Province of Georgia has the most ample and Satisfactory Protection by maintaining a Post at Savannah and another at Augusta, nor can I think myself justified in incurring any further expence [sic] on the Army Accounts for the Protection of Georgia."

The outline of the star-shaped fort at Ninety Six is still visible in the Ninety Six National Park. (Zachary Frank/Alamy)

The Siege of Mackay's Trading Post, September 14–18, 1780

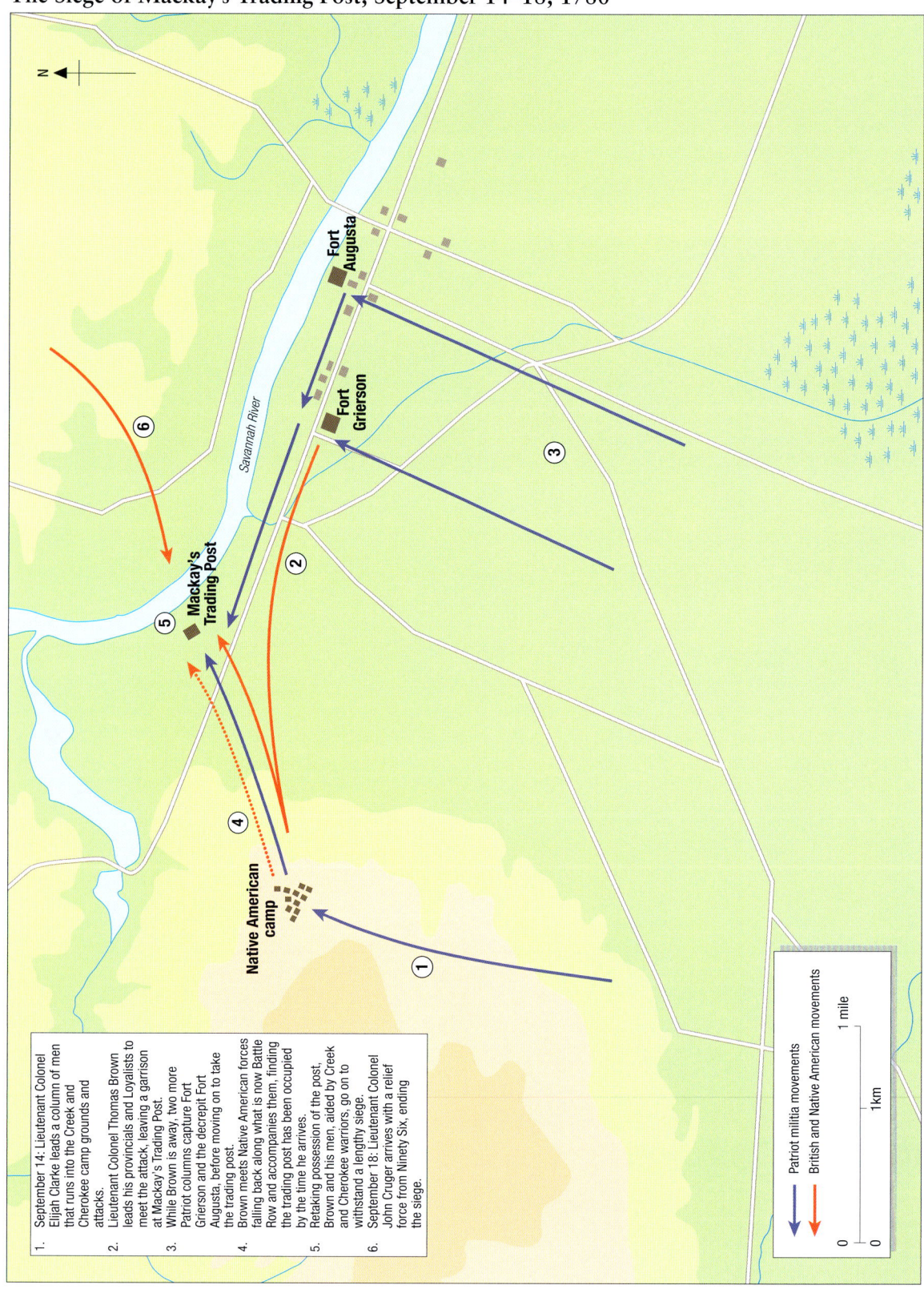

1. September 14: Lieutenant Colonel Elijah Clarke leads a column of men that runs into the Creek and Cherokee camp grounds and attacks.
2. Lieutenant Colonel Thomas Brown leads his provincials and Loyalists to meet the attack, leaving a garrison at Mackay's Trading Post.
3. While Brown is away, two more Patriot columns capture Fort Grierson and the decrepit Fort Augusta, before moving on to take the trading post.
4. Brown meets Native American forces falling back along what is now Battle Row and accompanies them, finding the trading post has been occupied by the time he arrives.
5. Retaking possession of the post, Brown and his men, aided by Creek and Cherokee warriors, go on to withstand a lengthy siege.
6. September 18: Lieutenant Colonel John Cruger arrives with a relief force from Ninety Six, ending the siege.

As a result of this, the only defensive work erected at Augusta was the pitifully small "Fort Grierson," which was nothing more than a modest stockade. Despite this, Brown had ambitious aims to maintain order in the colony, and threatened to hang any man, of any persuasion, who disturbed the peace by violence or robbery.

By August, the number of men he had to enforce this threat was down to 240 as illness nibbled away at his command, and there was a sense that trouble was brewing. Of particular concern was the fact that known Patriot leaders were living freely in the backcountry, and the fear was that these firebrands would eventually make a move. The Disqualifying Act (passed on July 1, 1780) had identified 155 such leaders, and imposed severe restrictions on them – they were not allowed to possess firearms, for example, or hold any public office. Having passed the act, however, nothing was done to enforce it, out of concern that draconian action might inflame a region that seemed calm.

The peacefulness of the region was debatable, and Lieutenant Colonel John Cruger, who had taken over at Ninety Six, was becoming concerned. He was receiving reports that Clarke was in Georgia, gathering men. It was believed he may have mustered as many as 300, and Cruger encouraged the disarming of at least the most committed Patriot leaders, a measure Brown wholeheartedly agreed with – but nothing was done, and the result was both bold and daring.

In September, Brown was taking part in a conference with Creek and Cherokee leaders when Clarke launched an ambitious assault on Augusta. Though caught completely off guard, Brown responded quickly. The first column of Clarke's men had attacked the Native American camp, about three miles outside of town, and Brown was soon on his way to fight off the attack, leaving a small garrison at Mackay's Trading Post en route.

The trading post, a white stone building, was being used to store the gifts that had been prepared for the tribes, valued at around £4,000. As he rushed to the Native Americans' assistance, Brown was unaware that Clarke's assault involved two further columns, and by the time he reached the Creek and Cherokee, these Patriots were entering the town unopposed, capturing Forts Augusta and Grierson, and then taking the trading post.

Having met the retreating Native Americans, Brown doubled back towards the town and was able to recapture the post, but then found himself besieged. If some of Clarke's men had not gone in search of plunder, it is possible the post would have fallen, but Brown was able to send a message out to Ninety Six and settled down to withstand a prolonged siege.

Clarke's attack was persistent. Over the following three days, his men cut off communications with the post and waited for Brown to surrender. As many as 300 of the Creek and Cherokee Brown had assisted at their camp stuck with the Loyalist commander, manning positions outside the building and fending off Clarke's men. During one lull in the fighting, a party of 50 Cherokee managed to get into the post, having swum the Savannah River.

Brown's men would have been envious of them, as there was no access to water inside the post, and Clarke's men ensured no parties could get through to the river to fill canteens. With the bodies of dead men and horses festering in the heat, and no drinking water, conditions in and around the trading post became hellish, and the garrison resorted to the desperate measure of drinking its own urine.

By the time Brown's messenger reached Cruger, the commander of Ninety Six was already preparing to march to Augusta's relief (Loyalists who had witnessed

THE SIEGE OF MACKAY'S TRADING POST, FIRST DAY, SEPTEMBER 14, 1780 (PP.40–41)

The owner of the main trading post at Augusta, Robert Mackay, had died in 1775, and it is believed to have been vacant at the time of the siege. It was being used to store the thousands of pounds' worth of gifts intended for the Creek and Cherokee as gestures of goodwill. The daring attack by Elijah Clarke exposed weaknesses in British intelligence gathering, as Thomas Brown admitted that he was "attacked by a Strong Body of Rebels – of whose march or movements I had not received the Smallest intimation till that moment."

Some of these rebels took possession of the trading post, and it had been thoroughly ransacked by the time the siege began. Clarke's men made good use of the many weapons included in the gifts, handing them out to more than 70 Patriot prisoners who had been released from Fort Augusta.

When Brown reached the trading post, finding it in rebel hands, he quickly re-established control: "After a Smart Conflict of Upwards an hour, we drove them from their ground, and from amongst the Houses where the Indian stores are lodged – and of which we immediately took possession – here we Continued engaged with them for I suppose full two hours longer, when they thought proper to retire."

During the firefight, Brown's men found cover in the trading post itself as well as in some of the outbuildings, while the Creek and Cherokee made use of a deep ditch outside the house **(1)**. Though sturdy, the trading post was vulnerable to rifle fire in places and many of the makeshift garrison received wounds during the most intense period of the fighting **(2)**. After nightfall, they would work on the defenses, curring loopholes into the walls to make it easier to return enemy fire, but during this initial engagement, Brown and his men had to risk showing themselves at the windows to fire on the Patriots **(3)**.

The Patriots also constructed sturdier positions as the siege progressed, digging a trench about 150 yards from the Creek and Cherokee position, but during this first firefight, they improvised as best they could, finding shelter behind trees or the occasional wagon **(4)**.

the opening shots of the battle had ridden to Ninety Six to alert the garrison). Leaving just a small force to hold the fort, Cruger set off on September 16, arriving two days later.

Clarke's men, already frustrated by the stubborn defense of the trading post, ran off as soon as they saw the relief column approaching. Native Americans set off in pursuit of the fleeing men, and Brown was able to capture a few who were too slow in making their escape. He discovered that many of the captured men had previously given their parole to the British. Being in violation meant their lives were forfeit, and Brown was in no mood for leniency.

Governor James Wright wrote with satisfaction of Brown's treatment of these men: "Thirteen of the Prisoners who broke their Parole and came against Augusta have been hang'd, which I hope will have a very Good Effect."

It did not have a good effect. Brown was demonized by the Patriots for his decision to hang the captured rebels, but the governor was in a particularly bloodthirsty mood following Clarke's raid. "The most Effectual and Best Method of Crushing the Rebellion in the Backs Parts of this Country," he claimed in a letter to Balfour, "is for an Army to march without Loss of time into the Ceded Lands – and to lay Waste and Destroy the whole Territory… for these People, the men have by their late conduct forfeited every claim to any favour or protection."

Wright's wishes were carried out. Around 100 of the men who had followed Clarke to Augusta watched as their homesteads were burned and their cattle confiscated. Loyalist militia, hungry for revenge, took many men prisoner and 23 were sent to Charleston. A good portion of the men in Clarke's force had left the region with him, but their families were not immune to Wright's vengeance. They too saw their homes destroyed and many had to attempt to catch up with their menfolk as they made their escape.

Belatedly, Brown was given authorization to build fortifications at Augusta. Fort Cornwallis was constructed on the site of the old Fort Augusta, and was completed in April 1781. It was considered an excellent fortification, but it would fall less than two months later, during another siege. Before that, Clarke's retreating men would have an influence on events leading up to Kings Mountain. As the British attempted to ensure that none of them escaped, the man best placed to cut off their retreat was Patrick Ferguson.

FERGUSON'S CAMPAIGN BEGINS

The area that Ferguson was leading his men into had experienced its share of violence. The defeat of the Cherokee in 1761 had opened up the possibility for more extensive settlement, and the Carolinas had split along an east–west divide. The East was politically dominant, while the West was considered backward and savage, with a reputation for often lethal disorder.

In 1767, an especially serious outbreak of violence in the South Carolina backcountry had led to the formation of the "Regulators" – vigilantes who numbered as many as 6,000 at their peak. At first, they were concerned with rooting out criminals, but they were later corrupted by their own power, helped by the fact that they were so far distant from the 'civilized' East. North Carolina had its own Regulator movement, but it had been defeated by

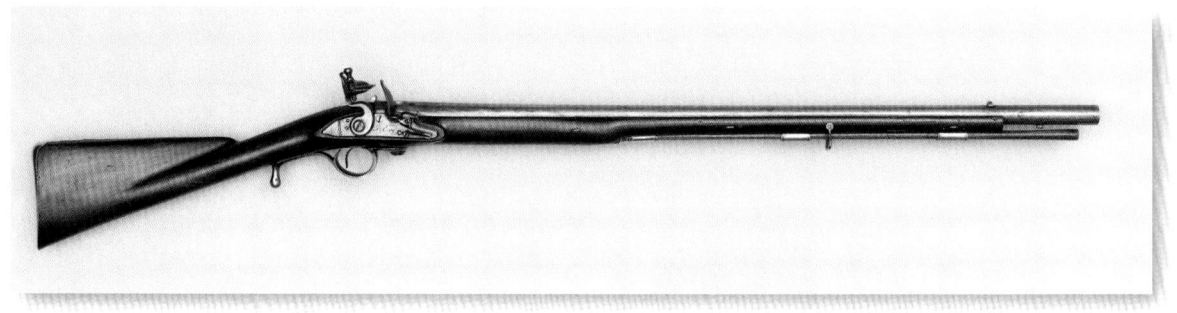

A 1776 version of the Ferguson rifle, manufactured by Durs Egg. The rifle was a third lighter than the standard British musket of the day. (© Royal Armouries)

Governor Tryon in 1771 at Alamance. Disgruntled Regulators then decided to get even further away from the political centers of their colonies, and moved over the mountains into lands that would later become known as the "Watauga Country." Here they set up the Watauga Association – effectively an independent system of government. For the most part, those who had chosen to live over the mountains were indifferent to the war, being more concerned with their own problems. Land was often ceded to the settlers by the Native American tribes, but this did not prevent some Native leaders from resenting the presence of homesteads on their territory.

Indifference to the war did not mean there had been no violence. In her evocative description of the period, Wilma Dykeman described the South as slipping into "a cannibalistic kind of fury" as Tory and Whig wrestled each other to death and many of the "outliers" (those loyal to neither cause) exploited the chaos for their own gain. In an area described by the historian Ian Saberton as "a powder keg waiting to explode," Ferguson was about to provide a spark.

The British commander had rejoined his men, following his conference with Cornwallis on the forthcoming campaign, on September 1. He subsequently crossed the border into North Carolina on September 7, the same day Cornwallis swung into action from Camden. It was a gamble, partly because of the perilously scanty garrisons being left behind to maintain control in Georgia and South Carolina, but also because the premise for the campaign was once more built on the flimsy foundations of supposed Loyalist support.

Cornwallis spelled this out in a letter to Wemyss, in which he admitted: "The object of marching into North Carolina is only to raise men, which, from every account I have received of the number of our friends, there is great reason to hope may be done to a very considerable amount."

Things got off to a bad start. On September 17, Tarleton fell ill with a nasty bout of yellow fever. Sickness was rife among the British troops but none were as indispensable as Cornwallis' mercurial British Legion commander. The British advance was slowed partly in response to this setback, which removed the most potent striking force from their arsenal. They did not enter Charlotte until September 26.

Wemyss had been engaged on his own mission, tasked by Cornwallis with pulling together Loyalist militia in the Cheraw District, east of Camden. His small, mounted corps (around 300 men in total, made up of elements of the 63rd Regiment, the Royal North Carolina Regiment, Harrison's Corps, and Bryan's militia) got to work burning the properties of those who had broken their parole. Men who had joined the Loyalist militia and then defected were ordered to be hanged, although Wemyss meted out this ultimate

Detail of the breech-loading mechanism of the Ferguson rifle, which allowed it to be fired up to six times a minute. (© Royal Armouries)

punishment to only one individual. His attempts to form a militia, however, were fruitless. The region was thoroughly anti-British, and any Loyalists that remained were completely cowed by their Patriot opponents. Wemyss' mission was a failure, but it did serve to further stoke up resentment to the British presence.

Cornwallis was aware of the difficulties involved in trying to bring the colony back to the Crown. "It is absolutely necessary to inflict some exemplary punishment on the [Patriot] militia and inhabitants of that part of the country," he had written to Colonel Francis, Lord Rawdon back in August. "On the moment we advance, we shall find an enemy in our rear... some force must be sent to reduce and intimidate that country or the communication between the upper army and Charlestown [sic] will be impracticable."

More success was enjoyed by Captain James Moncrief, who left Charleston on September 4 and retook control of Georgetown. The spine of his unit was made up of a mounted detachment of the 7th (Royal) Fusiliers, but he also had militia units and recruited new men along the way. Once Georgetown had been taken, he left the militia to hold the area and took his mounted fusiliers to Camden, but his success proved fleeting. Although Moncrief had at least been able to raise more militia, they were no match for Marion's partisans. Georgetown was back in American hands by the end of September, the Loyalist militia having been scattered.

Ferguson's men were not pleased to hear that they would be operating on the wing of Cornwallis' army rather than with the main body. Anthony Allaire wrote in his diary: "Maj. Ferguson rejoined us again from Camden with the disagreeable news that we were to be separated from the army, and act on the frontiers with the militia."

Why Allaire found this news so disagreeable was not revealed, but it is possible he had doubts about the abilities of the militia with them at the time and was concerned at the prospect of being detached from the main army, with all the dangers that entailed.

On September 2, the corps got under way at 1100hrs, marching 10 miles to Lawson's Fork on the Pacolet River. Allaire reported finding a former Patriot militiaman there, who had undergone an amputation after taking a musket ball to the arm in a skirmish at Cedar Springs a month earlier.

"It [the arm] was taken off by one Frost, a blacksmith, with a shoemaker's knife and carpenter's saw," Allaire noted, with evident approval of the skill demonstrated. "He stopped the blood with the fungus of the oak, without taking up a blood vessel."

Another 10-mile march followed on September 4, but on the 5th, having started out at 1700hrs, they managed just a mile and a half before finding the Pacolet River too high to cross. The next day, they marched six miles and were entertained by a 109-year-old New Englander who was still fit enough to dance a jig for his guests.

At this point, Ferguson had only 650 militia with him, which he described as "old and infirm." Some of them were not even armed or trained, casting doubt on the whole enterprise. He was awaiting the return of some of his younger men from furlough and, with this in mind, he admitted that he had "proceeded with more caution than would otherwise have been necessary." The small distances noted in Allaire's diary bear this out.

The British commander was making use of spies to get a picture of the area into which he was marching, and these assured him that there were no sizeable enemy forces to the east, which encouraged him to risk splitting his command. Taking 100 mounted militia and 50 mounted regulars, followed by 200 militia infantry, he marched to Gilbert Town, leaving DePeyster in command of the remainder of his corps. The place hardly deserved to be called a town, consisting of a single house, a blacksmith's, and a scattering of outbuildings, but Ferguson had heard that a small party of Patriots was in the area. He managed to capture a dozen men from Lieutenant Colonel Wade Hampton's militia unit (a regiment of light dragoons) and it was then that he learned of a party of Georgia militia under Elijah Clarke. Although Clarke was heading for Augusta, it was believed he had his sights set on Ninety Six and word was sent back to DePeyster to be on the alert in case Clarke's men ran into them.

Hampton had only had 60 men with him, and Clarke reportedly had just 100, but word was received that Charles McDowell was close with a larger force and that Shelby was expected to join him with 200 more.

Ferguson fell back on the remainder of his corps, hoping that he might draw McDowell into an attack. For a while it looked like this might have worked, as McDowell was reported as having advanced into a mountain pass. Ferguson immediately attempted to trap the Patriot force, taking 40 regulars and 100 militia on a march to get behind McDowell. The detachment left camp at 0200hrs on the morning of September 12, but it appears that McDowell in turn received intelligence about his opponent's movements, because he quickly left camp with his 300 militia. The two parties then blundered into each other – while some of Ferguson's men were pursuing a small number of partisans, McDowell's force appeared only 100 or so yards away, descending a slope. McDowell quickly turned about, climbed the slope and took up a strong position.

"To appearance one would have thought they meant sincerely to fight us," Allaire noted in his diary, "as they drew up on an eminence for action," but no serious engagement ensued. "After a few idle shots on their part, [they] gave way," Ferguson reported, "and their whole party fled

Wade Hampton served as a Member of Congress for South Carolina after the Revolution and was a general during the War of 1812. (Heritage Art/Heritage Images via Getty Images)

with little loss as our horses were jaded by [a] march of 30 miles and the country cover'd with wood." Two of McDowell's men had been killed and 17 captured, along with their horses and another horse carrying ammunition. Ferguson had lost one man killed and an officer and one militiaman wounded.

Ferguson now issued a declaration to the Patriots in the region. He chose several of his recently taken prisoners (the ones he deemed to be of "the most character and moderation") and sent them home to spread the word – he did not make it clear if they were provided with written copies, but it seems certain they merely carried the gist of the declaration to spread by word of mouth. The words bear serious consideration, because they are so strongly at odds with the infamous threat he is alleged to have issued to the Overmountain Men.

Dated September 9, the declaration began:

> The experience that the deluded inhabitants of the revolted American provinces have had of the falsehoods by which the rebel leaders have artfully excited them, against their duty to God and their King and their best interests, to involve their country in blood and misery will, it is hoped, by degrees open their eyes that they may at last listen to the calm voice of reason and truth.

Ferguson then went on to list and debunk a number of charges laid against the British in Patriot propaganda. He denied that Britain was planning to introduce Catholicism to the colonies, at the same time as pointing out that Congress had entered into treaties with Catholic nations. He denied the claim that Britain was intending to let Native Americans loose on the colonists "to murder and lay waste," pointing out that the Patriots had enrolled help from the Native Americans. He insisted that the British had always acted to restrain their Native allies and indeed to limit the actions of "bad men on both sides from aggravating the horrors of war by rapine and outrage."

He referred to rumors that the King planned to "enslave" his colonists, and pointed out that Britain had renounced the right to tax its colonies and to restore "all their antient rights and libertys to those Americans who should submit." He denied that those former Patriots in South Carolina who had accepted the offer of parole had been forced to enlist in the British forces (although it is clear that Clinton's ill-judged proclamation was at the heart of this rumor). Furthermore, he denied that the parolees had been systematically mistreated, insisting that every effort had been made to stop Loyalists from exacting vengeance for "the injuries that their innocent familys had suffer'd during the rebel government."

He then summed up his offer: "In a word, the King by proclamation, and in consequence of a solemn Act of His Parliament, holds forth to every American who is disposed to return to his duty an offer of the same free and happy government he formerly enjoy'd, with an exemption from taxation and pardon for all offences; and His officers are strictly commanded to protect to the utmost of their power all men who submit and all women and children of every denomination."

There was a little more talk of the futility of continuing a war when the outcome had already been decided, and disparaging mention of those men (with Clarke and Shelby hinted at) who continued to wage war having "got a habit of rapine and plunder." The population was promised hard cash in exchange for any stores required by the British Army, in contrast to the "waste paper" of American notes, and there was a final promise to all men – Patriot and Loyalist alike – that British troops would always protect their women and children, no matter what they decided to do.

It was a detailed and heartfelt proclamation, but it was doomed to fall flat. The high-handed tone of the declaration was not so much of a problem in an era where this was simply the style (Patriot proclamations were equally long-winded to modern ears). More important was the fact that the Patriots had no doubt the war was far from decided, felt they had no need to ask for forgiveness for their actions, and felt no sense of "duty" to a monarch who, in their minds, had outstayed his welcome. Moreover, many had direct experience of harsh and even brutal treatment from British soldiers and Loyalist militia, so talk of protecting their children and women sounded hollow.

The declaration of September 9 was therefore unlikely to sway any Patriot hearts (if indeed the chosen messengers managed to remember more than a few snippets of the lengthy message), but it did display a willingness on the part of Ferguson to attempt to win men over by reason. Lyman C. Draper noted, in his work on the Battle of Kings Mountain, that Ferguson would "sit down for hours, and converse with the country people… this condescension on his part was regarded as wonderful in a King's officer, and very naturally went far to secure the respect and obedience of all who came within the sphere of his almost magic influence."

A further declaration was issued to the Loyalists of Tryon County, entreating them not to rise until "called for by proper authority and supported." The painful results of Loyalists declaring their hand too early had been seen too often, and Ferguson did not want them to receive the same lesson again. At the same time, rewards of up to 100 guineas were offered to any man who could provide effective intelligence that enabled the British to defeat an enemy force.

This message to the Patriots is not often mentioned in histories of the Battle of Kings Mountain. Instead, another declaration is given precedence, a belligerent threat that is usually presented in exactly the same format. The words were first mentioned by Isaac Shelby himself, lending them credibility, but this was not until 1823, when he published a pamphlet on his wartime experiences and included the following passage:

> At that place he [Ferguson] paroled a prisoner, (one Samuel Philips a distant connection of mine) and instructed him to inform the officers on the Western waters, that if they did not desist from their opposition to the British arms, and take protection under his standard, he would march his army over the mountains, hang their leaders, and lay their country waste with fire and sword. Philips lived near my residence, and came directly to me with this intelligence.

This threat has been part of Kings Mountain lore for two centuries, but there was no mention of it prior to Shelby's 1823 pamphlet and there is serious doubt that Ferguson ever issued it. Details around the legend make it clear that the message was carried verbally, rather than in written form, which raises questions. Is it possible that Ferguson's original message, as detailed in his letter to Cornwallis, became distorted in transit? None of the written accounts of the battle by the actual participants mention this message in detail. The official report, published in November 1780, did say that Ferguson had "threatened to cross the mountains to the western waters," but no mention was made of him threatening to lay waste to the region. Such a threat would seem badly out of character for a man who prided himself in preferring the approach of persuasion and reason, but the legend cannot be totally dismissed – although it seems unlikely, it is at least possible that Ferguson did send the threatening message, but made no mention of it to his superior.

What is not in doubt is that Ferguson sent some sort of message. The Overmountain Men were aware of his presence – they almost certainly had been already, given his proximity and his clashes with Patriot militia in the area – and in response to this threat, their leaders held a meeting.

THE MUSTER AT SYCAMORE SHOALS

The area over the mountains had long been shrouded in mystery. When Lord Rawdon wrote his report on the Battle of Kings Mountain, he mentioned that an army had come together from "settlements beyond the mountains whose very names had been unknown to us."

Shelby kickstarted the process of gathering the Overmountain Men together, riding 40 miles to the house of John Sevier, in the Nolichucky Valley. In Shelby's later account of events, this was in response to the "fire and sword" threat issued by Ferguson, but it may have followed receipt of the more measured declaration detailed in Ferguson's letter to Cornwallis. Whatever brought the two Patriot commanders together,

The Abingdon Muster Grounds, where hundreds of Virginians met prior to marching to Sycamore Shoals. (Overmountain Victory National Historic Trail)

THE MUSTER OF THE OVERMOUNTAIN MEN, SEPTEMBER 25, 1780 (PP.50–51)

The muster at Sycamore Shoals was a rare event, bringing together people from the scattered settlements over the mountains. Although they shared a common purpose, these were men who were used to making their own decisions and living in isolation – there were inevitable flashpoints as so many of them rubbed shoulders. Old grudges might be brought up and rehashed, although it appears the muster was mainly peaceful as the men remained focused on their goal **(1)**. A Loyalist officer, speaking after the disaster at Kings Mountain, commented that "[these were] the most powerful men ever beheld, tall, rawboned, sinewy, from the extreme backwoods… whom no labor could tire and whose rifles seldom missed their mark."

The gathering would have allowed for the usual exchange of news, the showing off of new weapons **(2)**, and the chance to share a meal, prepared by women who had no idea if their menfolk would be returning from this adventure **(3)**. Young men, some as young as 15, might be counseled by an older family member and encouraged to do their best during the trying times ahead **(4)**. Although many of the gathered men were without horses, only those with sturdy mounts would make it to the end of the long and grueling march, as the cream of the small army would be picked for the final push to catch up with Ferguson and his Loyalist force **(5)**.

they decided it would be in their best interests to take offensive action against Ferguson.

The support of William Campbell (commanding the Washington County Regiment from Virginia) was considered critical, but he was initially skeptical about crossing the mountains in pursuit of Ferguson, arguing that it made more sense to stay put and force the British commander to come to them. With Shelby and Sevier insisting the expedition could not take place without him, Campbell was persuaded to take part and would eventually become the expedition's overall commander. Charles McDowell (with militia from Burke and Rutherford Counties, North Carolina), also agreed to join, and a call went out for men to gather at Sycamore Shoals, on the Watauga River.

The little matter of financing a serious military expedition was dealt with quickly. John Adair, the "entry taker" of Sullivan County, had collected the payments for land taken on by settlers, and he agreed to give it up as a loan. Around $12,000 was thus made available and the region became a hive of activity as clothes, food, and ammunition were prepared.

On September 25, the Overmountain Men began to assemble at Sycamore Shoals. McDowell's men, around 160 strong, had been present for several days already, following their brushes with Ferguson, but McDowell himself was away, gathering support for the expedition. Sevier and Shelby each brought around 240 men, while Colonel Arthur Campbell brought 200 Virginians and immediately headed back to find more.

A gathering on such a scale was a novelty, and inevitably the close proximity of men and families who were more used to living in isolation prompted excitement and a few arguments. There was the promise of violence in the air, and there was also anxiety over the fact that so many men would be leaving their homesteads for a significant period of time. The very young and elderly would remain behind, but it would be important to get the expedition over with as quickly as possible. Around 1,000 men had gathered, as well as many families, and the day was imagined in evocative terms by Wilma Dykeman when she wrote:

> As they assembled—more than 1,000 strong, the largest gathering of settlers that had ever been seen in that part of the country—they built their campfires, smelled the bitter pungence of wood smoke in the evening air and the welcome aromas of food, and tended the beeves [cows] they were taking along for a ready food supply. The men talked and planned and prepared.

The small army, formidable though it was in many ways, had an inbuilt weakness. There was no overall commanding officer, each group of men owing allegiance only to their own officers. They would work together in pursuit of a higher goal, but only as long as the commanders of each faction were in agreement. At any moment an argument or disagreement might fracture the force, and the longer they were in the field, the stronger the lure of their homesteads would become, and the greater the potential for rifts. They would need to find and deal with Ferguson quickly, and just as they were aware of his presence, he was very much aware of them.

On September 19, Ferguson had written to Cornwallis, mentioning rumors that the "back-water men" were gathering in substantial numbers. He mentioned that 800, under Shelby, were planning to cross over the mountains,

"The Gathering of the Overmountain Men at Sycamore Shoals," by Lloyd Branson. (Lloyd Branson (painter), public domain, via Wikimedia Commons)

but did not appear to be in the least concerned. He had sent another messenger, this time to find the retreating McDowell, with more promises that any men who gave up their struggle would be generously treated.

Three days later, he again mentioned intelligence of Patriot militia coming together. This time he had more details, and reported that the combined force was expected to pass through the "Flower Gap" in the mountains, to menace settlements on the head of the New River. He mentioned "Campbell" and "English," but it is unclear to where he was referring.

Ferguson's intelligence, though inaccurate in detail, was correct in one respect – the Overmountain Men were on the move. Wasting no time after assembling, they broke camp on the morning of September 26 and started their march. George Hanger may have noted that clergymen were as rare as angels in the backcountry, but one was present during the muster at Sycamore Shoals – Reverend Samuel Doak delivered a tub-thumping speech, which is believed to have ended with the rallying cry of "The sword of the Lord and of Gideon."

The men set off, but were hampered by their slow-moving beef cattle. Tradition has it they camped at Shelving Rock on the Little Doe River that first night and by the following morning they had already lost patience with their walking food store. They slaughtered some of the cattle and abandoned the rest, before setting out to cross the mountains.

An ensign in the party, Robert Campbell, noted the crossing in his diary. Following a well-known mountain trail, Bright's Trace, they moved through a gap between Yellow Mountain and Roan Mountain. According to Campbell's diary, as the men climbed, "they found the sides and top of the mountain covered with snow, shoe-mouth deep; and on the summit, there were about 100 acres of beautiful table-land, in which a spring issued, ran through it, and over into the Watauga."

The summit, known as "the Bald Place" or "the Bald of the Yellow," made a convenient spot for the men to parade under the eyes of their commanding officers. It was also the point where two of Sevier's men decided this was as far as they were willing to go. James Crawford and

Sycamore Shoals, on the banks of the Watauga River. (Dee Browning/Alamy)

Samuel Chambers deserted, and their absence was soon noted. Although it was possible they had simply decided they did not want to be a part of the expedition anymore, it was more likely that they intended to deliver a warning to Ferguson. With the knowledge that the British commander might soon be informed of the approach of more than 1,000 men, it was even more imperative to move quickly. Four more miles were covered that afternoon, taking them as far as Elk Hollow, where they camped for the night. The next day, they covered 20 miles over difficult and rocky terrain, although the surrounding scenery was spectacular, and the weather was described as very mild.

By then, Ferguson was receiving reports of widespread Patriot activity. Oblivious to the fact that he was the focus of it, he wrote to Cornwallis from his camp near Gilbert Town, on September 28, that his command was "in the center of a variety of rebel parties." He listed various small gatherings of troops, but was completely unaware that a large body was on his trail. The possibility of a conjunction of the various groups listed had occurred to him, but he believed that the target of such a large, combined force would be elsewhere.

"It would seem that all these small partys were meant to have join'd and form'd a pretty powerfull diversion towards 96," he informed Cornwallis, "upon the supposition that the troops there would have had enough ado on the side of Augusta…"

With that in mind, he considered the defeat of Elijah Clarke to have been welcome in more ways than one – not only had he failed to take Augusta, the garrison of Ninety Six would be free to tackle any large body of militia on its way to them. He also displayed no concern whatsoever at being in the middle of various bodies of hostile troops. In fact, he considered his position to be "rather lucky. We shall be ready for to strike at whatever comes within our reach, and situated centrical as we are, I shall think us unfortunate if we do not prevent a general junction and remain masters of the field."

Roaring Creek Valley, site of Elk Hollow, one of the camping points on the march of the Overmountain Men. (Overmountain Victory National Historic Trail)

Ferguson's misapprehension of his situation was understandable – he was receiving snippets of intelligence from various sources and attempting to fit them together into a coherent picture – but it was disastrous. Far from being in a position to prevent a conjunction of Patriot units, that conjunction had taken place days earlier, and it had not been for the goal of attacking Ninety Six. As the small Patriot army made its way towards Quaker Meadows, Ferguson sat and waited, unaware of the mounting danger. "[I]n the present circumstances it appears to me improper to turn our backs on this frontier for some days," he informed Cornwallis, patiently waiting for small numbers of the enemy to fall into his lap.

By now, he was aware of reports that Shelby was on his way with 800 "Back Water" men, but he doubted the actual number would be greater than 300. He made a request for 200 mounted infantry and the British Legion to mount a diversionary action for three days, "towards Little Broad River," with the aim of dispersing all Patriots in the area.

The movements of Ferguson's force had been limited and uneventful. On the 25th and 26th, Allaire recorded in his diary that they had not strayed from their camp at Gilbert Town. On the 27th, they marched just three miles and the following day a total of about 12 miles in several bursts. The reason for this lack of urgency was noted by Allaire – they were loitering with intent, believing that they could intercept Clarke on his return from Augusta. This decision, which rooted Ferguson's command in place for days, was to have dire consequences.

Ferguson's intelligence was about to receive a significant boost. On September 30, he reported that six men had arrived with information. Two of them claimed to have been at the "rebels' muster" the previous Monday, September 25. It is possible that these were the two men who had deserted from the Patriot force two days after that, but they made no mention of having started on the march from Sycamore Shoals – Ferguson reported that they had left the Patriots at Sycamore Shoals before the main force had set off. Whoever they were, their information brought the other scattered pieces of intelligence into sharper focus.

The road to Kings Mountain, September 25–October 1, 1780

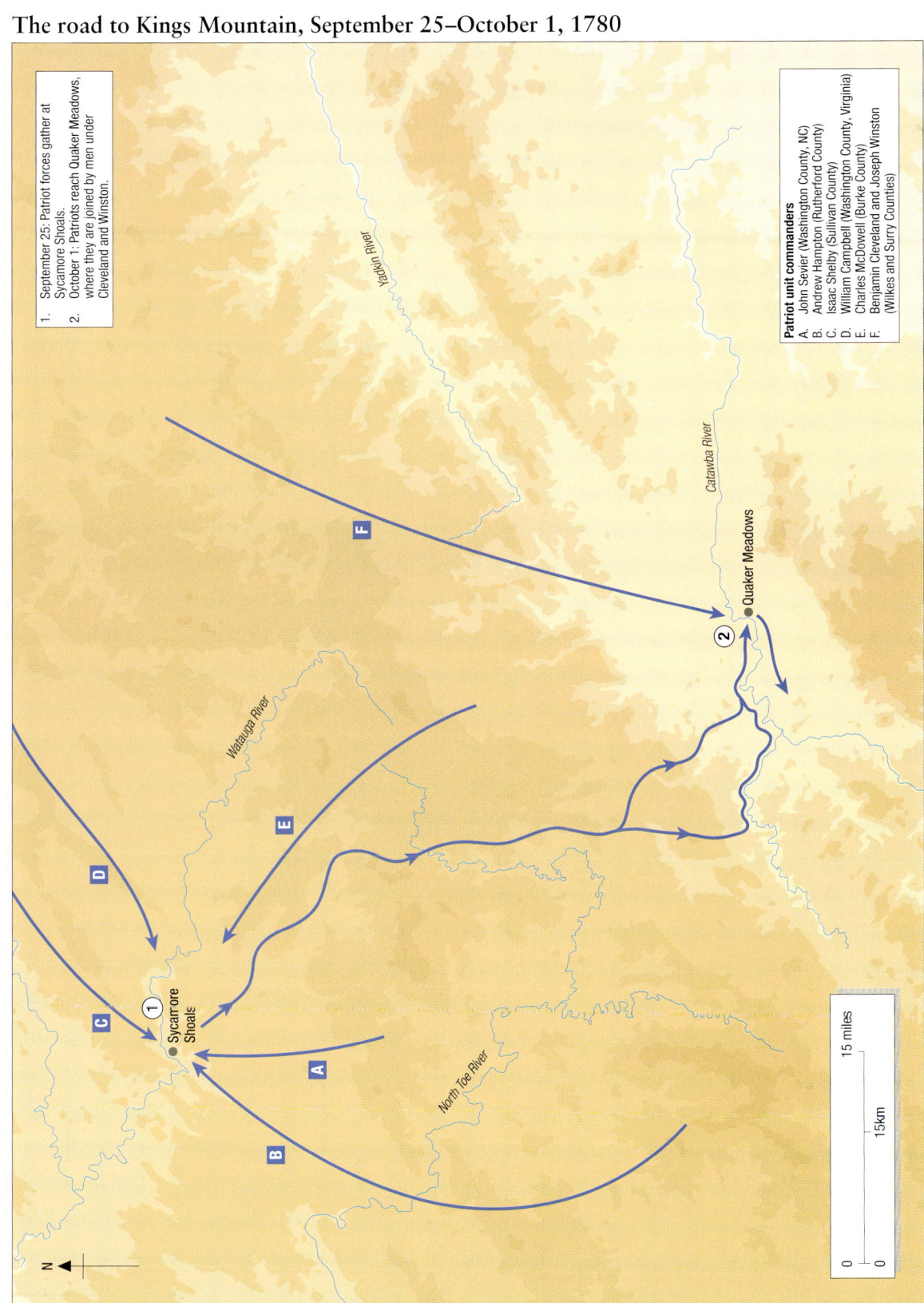

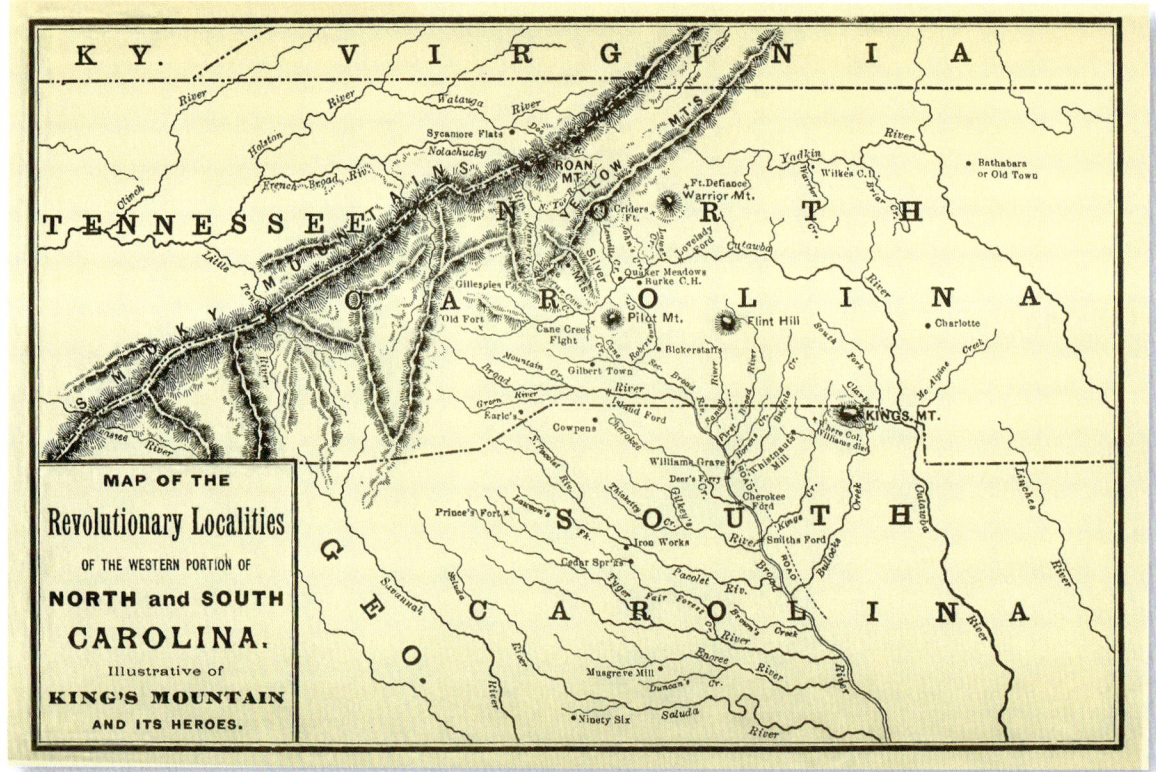

"Map of the Revolutionary Localities of the Western Portion of North and South Carolina." (From *King's Mountain and its Heroes* by Lyman Draper)

The deserters reported that "McDowel and Shelvy" had gathered men together with a view to returning across the mountains. This force was reckoned to be about 1,000 strong and was expected to have crossed the mountains by the Sunday (October 1). Worryingly, there was mention of another 500 men, under General (actually Colonel) Benjamin Cleveland, approaching to link up with Shelby's force once they had crossed the mountains. Ferguson obviously took pains to determine if this was reliable intelligence or not, reporting to Cornwallis that, "I have examin'd the people from Nolachucki [Nolichucky] and am of the opinion the accounts are to be credited."

The sobering news did not dampen Ferguson's optimism. He made no mention of believing that his own command was the target of Shelby's force, but it would have been peculiar if the deserters had not mentioned that critical piece of information. Rather than seeing danger, Ferguson saw an opportunity and again requested assistance from the British Legion, which would, he believed, allow them to secure an important victory.

"If the diversion of the Legion or even one half of it would take place for a few days," he wrote, "the happiest opportunity offers of crushing the Back Mountain men, who cannot at other times be reach'd and [may] be a serious thorn in the rear of your army, and have it at all times in their power to be a formidable support to the malcontents and bring this district into danger."

Underlining the fact that he did not consider himself to be under any threat, he informed Cornwallis that he would hold his current position for another two days in hopes of intercepting Clarke, but would then move eastwards. The following day, October 1, Ferguson marched his men to Denard's Ford, where they had been back on September 8. As the crow flies, the Patriots were now just 35 miles away.

The 1,000-strong Patriot force had reached Quaker Meadows in five days, pushing themselves hard in the knowledge that Ferguson was soon likely to be warned about their presence. Had they been aware of the British commander's lack of concern over their numbers, they might have taken a more leisurely approach.

While resting at the plantation owned by Major Joseph McDowell, their numbers were swelled by 400 men under the command of Cleveland and Joseph Winston. With such a sizeable force, and with so many factions, there was now a real danger of confusion and dissent. On October 2, a meeting of all commanding officers determined that an overall leader was needed. McDowell was the senior officer, but Shelby was concerned that he was not energetic enough to be effective in the position. In his pamphlet, written in 1823, he expanded upon his thinking at the time: "He was a brave and patriotic man, but we considered him too far advanced in life, and too inactive for the command of such an enterprise as we were engaged in." It is worth noting that McDowell was only 37 years old at the time, but he was sent to ask Horatio Gates if he would provide the small army with a general. The request was never likely to receive a swift response, but it got McDowell out of the way without any hint of disgrace. Knowing that there was no chance of a suitable general being sent to them in time, William Campbell (the only officer present who was not from North Carolina) was selected as the overall commander. It was in many ways a nominal command only, as the colonels met every day to decide on their next move.

Joseph Winston was awarded a sword by the Legislature of North Carolina for his conduct at Kings Mountain. (From *King's Mountain and its Heroes* by Lyman Draper)

It was October 5 before Cornwallis was able to respond to Ferguson's correspondence from the end of September. In a brief message, he advised Ferguson to move his men to Armer's [Armour's] Ford, close to Charlotte. It was a clear indication that he felt Ferguson was in danger and also a damning indictment of the overall British plan – Ferguson was meant to be clearing the backcountry and screening the main army. Instead, Cornwallis was calling him close so that he could be protected from the gathering Patriot militia.

Ferguson would not receive Cornwallis' message in time, but his confidence was already beginning to slowly erode as further news reached him. Having written to his commanding officer in fairly buoyant mood on September 30, he struck a different tone the following day. He reported that he now had intelligence that the "Back Water" men had already crossed the mountains, numbering around 800, with more detachments on the way to join them. He mentioned that Clarke appeared to have given him the slip and now felt the need to "play off a little and incline eastward if push'd." (It is worth noting that Clarke's retreating force had no goal but to cross the mountains to safety, but around 30 of his men, under Major Candler and Captain Johnston, joined Shelby's command.)

Ferguson then made an enigmatic statement, saying that no word had been received from Lieutenant Colonel Cruger at Ninety Six. Was Ferguson

Major Joseph McDowell, who commanded the Burke County Regiment while his elder brother Charles was on a mission to find a general for the Patriot force. (From *King's Mountain and its Heroes* by Lyman Draper)

beginning to feel his isolation? Two days later, more detail was added. He revealed that he had written to Cruger to ask for a reinforcement of 100 men. There was also a hint of back-covering when he claimed to have lingered to scoop up Clarke "by desire of Colonel Cruger."

Having been oblivious to the gathering danger for so long, Ferguson was suddenly seeing it everywhere. "The accounts I sent your Lordship respecting the Back Mountain men... have been confirm'd from various quarters and they are probably by this time reinforced by Sumter, Grahame's or Clark, if not by all," he informed Cornwallis. Ferguson was now apprehensive that every Patriot force in the region was coalescing. He tried to put on a brave face, claiming he would beat them if the numbers were "within bounds," but he also asked for 400 dragoons and the same number of mounted infantry, adding that the Loyalist units in the South Forks would be welcome.

"As it is," he concluded, "we shall act with caution and perhaps rather allow them to distress a few farms than fight prematurely."

Ferguson was deluding himself if he believed the Overmountain Men had come merely to distress a few farms. His level of concern was further revealed by a desperate plea to local Loyalists to turn out in his support:

> Gentlemen: Unless you wish to be eat up by an inundation of barbarians, who have begun by murdering an unarmed son before his aged father, and afterwards lopped off his arms, and who by their shocking cruelties and irregularities, give the best proof of their cowardice and want of discipline; I say, if you want to be pinioned, robbed, and murdered, and see your wives and daughters, in four days, abused by the dregs of mankind–in short, if you wish to deserve to live, and bear the name of men, grasp your arms in a moment and run to camp. The Back Water men have crossed the mountains; McDowell, Hampton, Shelby, and Cleveland are at their head, so that you know what you have to depend upon. If you choose to be degraded forever and ever by a set of mongrels, say so at once, and let your women turn their backs upon you, and look out for real men to protect them.

It is clear from his appeal that Ferguson was feeling pressured, but it remains a mystery why he did not move quickly towards Charlotte for protection. He may have feared that it would look cowardly to run for the protective wing of the main army at the first sign of danger, but had he known about Cornwallis' suggestion to move to Armour's Ford he would have been able to reach safety with some ease. Another possibility is worthy of consideration – Ferguson did not want to admit that he was not able to accomplish the task set to him as part of Cornwallis' overall plan. As a champion of the Loyalist

The road to Kings Mountain, October 1–7, 1780

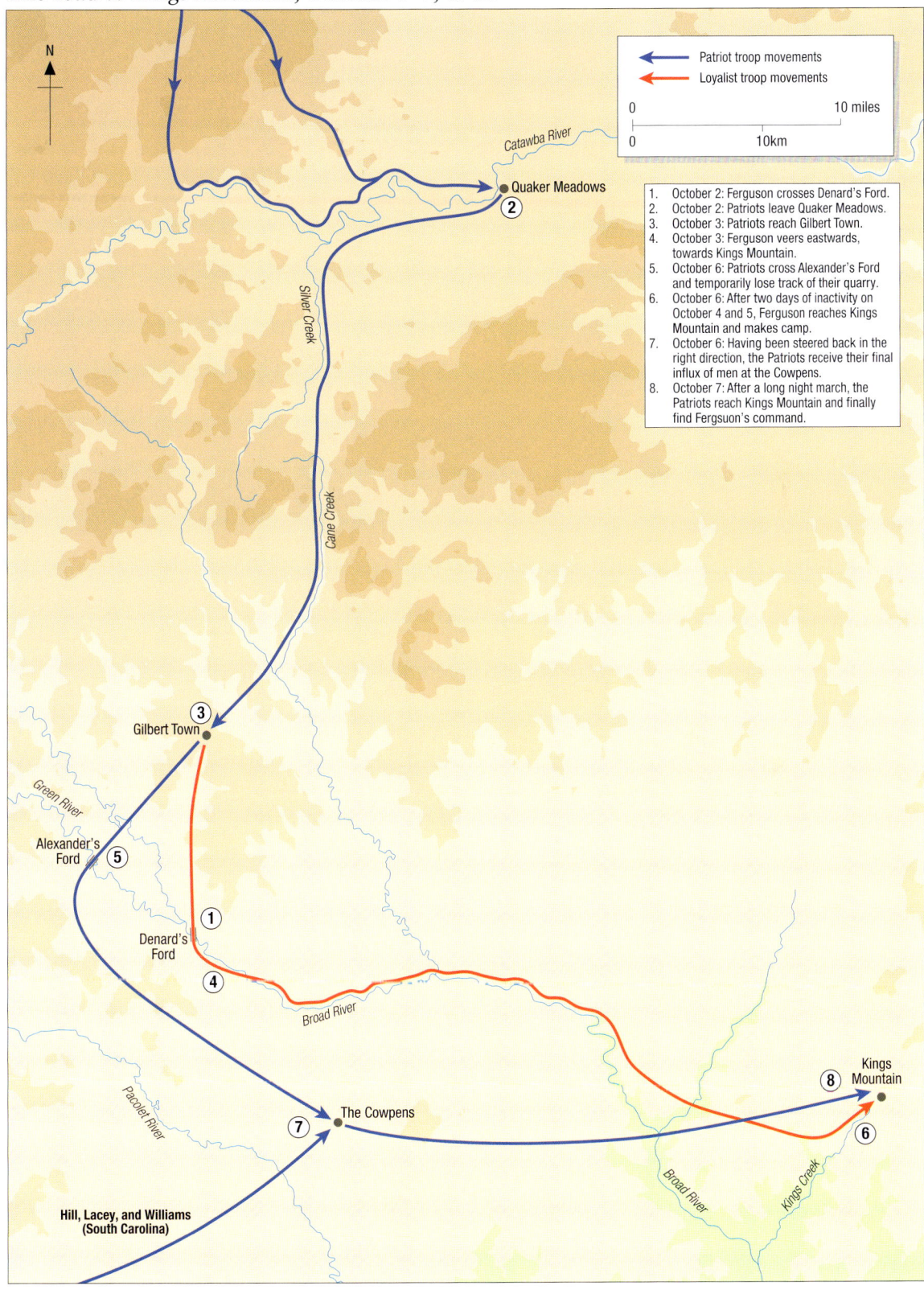

militia, and especially of those under his command, it would have been galling to admit that a sizeable Patriot force had made him turn tail and run.

Showing all the signs of being uncertain of how to proceed, Ferguson did not break camp until 1600hrs on October 2, and he marched just four miles, including the crossing of Broad River, before setting up camp again. His instincts may have been telling him conflicting things – he sensed the danger of the gathering Patriot force, but also an opportunity to show that his militia could fight on equal terms. It is also possible that he believed the Patriots were already closing in at this point. Allaire reported that the men "formed in line of action and lay on our arms" at the end of the march on October 2, suggesting that Ferguson believed an engagement was imminent.

In contrast, the next day was a flurry of activity. Allaire reported that they were on their way at 0400hrs and marched 20 miles. The same day, the Patriots reached Gilbert Town, hoping to find Ferguson still there. Prior to moving out the day before, clearly also thinking that an engagement was at hand, Shelby had given the men a few stirring words.

"When we encounter the enemy," he had explained, "don't wait for the word of command. Let each one of you be your own officer, and do the very best you can, taking every care you can of yourselves, and availing yourselves of every advantage that chance may throw in your way."

It was a pragmatic and sensible instruction. Unaccustomed as the men were to taking orders, there was little sense in anyone issuing them. After reaching Gilbert Town, however, there was a fear that their quarry had eluded them. Ferguson was not there, and the Patriot commanders were also having to deal with varied and often conflicting snippets of intelligence. Reports came in that the Loyalists were at least 50 miles away. Another report claimed they were heading to Ninety Six, where they would be all but untouchable behind the fortifications there. It appeared as if all the hardships of the long march so far may have been for nothing.

THE FINAL REINFORCEMENTS

At the same time as the main Patriot force was pursuing Ferguson, a second body was assembling. James Williams was a controversial figure at the time and the controversy continues today. Promoted to brigadier general of the South Carolina militia following his part in the successful Battle of Ramsour's Mill, he was unpopular with the followers of Thomas Sumter, who believed Williams had exaggerated his part in the victory and downplayed or even failed to mention that of Sumter. Sumter himself was absent from his command in the run-up to Kings Mountain, arguing his case to be promoted above Williams.

On October 2, Williams had moved his small regiment to Beattie's Ford, where they were joined by 100 mounted men under Colonel William Graham and Lieutenant Colonel William Hambright. Another 60 men, under Colonel Benjamin Roebuck, Lieutenant Colonel James Hawthorn, Major Samuel Hammond, and Major William Chronicle, joined later that day.

At Beattie's Ford, Williams came across a 270-strong party of Sumter's men, commanded by Colonels William Hill and Edward Lacey. Here, the story becomes unclear. The bad blood between Williams and Sumter meant his appearance was unwelcome. Williams, believing that his commission as a general gave him the right to command the combined force, was disabused of this notion in forthright terms by Lacey and Hill. As a result, the two bodies remained separate, although taking roughly parallel paths.

In a letter to General Gates, Williams outlined the position as far as he knew it – he had 450 mounted men with him (it appears he was including Sumter's men in this number, despite their hostility towards him), McDowell and Shelby had 1,500 men around Burke Court House, and Cleveland was expected to join them there with 800. Williams hoped to join up with this larger body the following day, but that was to prove wishful thinking.

The story then becomes decidedly murky. Lacey would claim that Williams secretly rode to the main body of Patriots under Campbell and informed them that Ferguson was heading for Ninety Six. Williams himself was from that district, and the implication was that he wanted to draw the Patriot force there to take control of the territory and plunder the local Tories. With this in mind, a meeting between the two groups of Patriots had been agreed for the Old Iron Works on Lawson's Fork, which would have been directing the main Patriot force away from Ferguson and towards Ninety Six. Had Williams deliberately tried to draw the Patriots away from Ferguson to serve his own ends in the region of Ninety Six? The truth is not clear, but there would be a final twist to cap off the controversy.

Tracking Ferguson, the main body of Patriots under Campbell missed the point where Ferguson had swung to the east. As well as the trail going cold, the Patriots were slowing as men and horses began to break down from the rigors of the march. They covered around 13 miles on October 5 and decided that a change of plan was required.

Samuel Hammond fought at Point Pleasant during Lord Dunmore's War and was a Continental Army officer in Virginia before moving to South Carolina in 1779. (From *King's Mountain and its Heroes* by Lyman Draper)

Detailed as "Ferguson's Headquarters," this may be a fair representation of one of the homesteads visited by the British commander on his way to Kings Mountain. (From *King's Mountain and its Heroes* by Lyman Draper)

At this point in the course of events, confusion enters the picture. It is never easy to be certain of troop numbers when militia are involved and that is especially true in such a dynamic situation as this, where the army was frequently joined by bodies of troops of varying sizes, but things were about to become even more complicated. Needing to increase their speed, the Patriots were about to make two adjustments to their force during their final approach to Kings Mountain.

The slow rate of progress was a problem, but so too was the increasing fatigue of the men, who had now been on the march for 10 days with no sign of catching Ferguson and would start to lose interest in the operation soon. The eccentric progress of the British commander was also problematic, but this was about to be addressed very neatly – an elderly Patriot had managed to get into Ferguson's camp. Putting on a convincing display of loyalism, the man apparently managed to gather useful intelligence on the British commander's intentions. The veracity of this story is obviously questionable – whether Ferguson or his officers would have been loose-lipped with a stranger seems unlikely – but the events that followed appear to support it. The elderly gentleman is credited with travelling 20 miles on the night of October 4 to arrive at the camp of Sumter's men, where he made a report to Hill and Lacey.

Now having solid intelligence of Ferguson's position and intended route of march, Lacey set off to inform Campbell and hopefully persuade him not to march for the Old Iron Works. According to his own account, Lacey left camp around 2000hrs on the night of October 5. His mission to alert Campbell's men to the whereabouts of Ferguson took on some hair-raising elements, which may have been added to embellish the story in retrospect. He claimed to have been suspected as a Loyalist spy and taken to Campbell wearing a blindfold, but eventually a meeting place more suited to the pursuit of Ferguson was agreed upon – the Cowpens.

Alexander's Ford, on the Green River, where the Patriots rested on the night of October 5, prior to crossing the next day. (Overmountain Victory National Historic Trail)

The morning of October 6 proved critical. Williams allegedly attempted to get the South Carolinians on the march towards the Old Iron Works before Lacey had returned from his conference with Campbell. Hill vigorously opposed his attempts and their men were left to wonder what the proper course of action was, with two officers shouting contradictory orders at them. The return of Lacey, around 1000hrs, settled the matter. The men would march to the Cowpens.

While Lacey had been riding back to his camp, the main Patriot force was reorganizing itself for a final dash to catch Ferguson. Only the men with the strongest horses were selected to push forwards, with the remainder, and those on foot, following as best they could. Around 700 were selected. As soon as the sun rose on October 6, this streamlined army began to move towards the Cowpens, covering the 21 miles before sunset. On the way, they moved close to a Loyalist force under Zacharias Gibbs, which was on its way to join with Ferguson. This corps, numbering between 400 and 600, might have made a decisive impact on the course of the battle to come, and the failure of Gibbs to reach Ferguson has been a controversial point. An explanation was unearthed in the form of letters received from Ferguson that were included in Gibbs' compensation application following the war.

Ferguson's letters show that he was concerned that smaller bodies of Loyalists, in trying to reach him, might stumble upon the large Patriot force and be destroyed piecemeal. On October 5, he had written to Gibbs: "Sir I am now on my march to [illegible word] near King's Mountain. I wish not to have any reinforcements from you immediately as they may be Destroyed on their way. take Care of yourself—for some Days—Sumpter & Clark have joined Macdowal." Gibbs, therefore, appears to have been exonerated for his failure to link up with Ferguson.

Upon their arrival at the Cowpens, some sources assert that the main Patriot force found the South Carolinians (under Hill, Lacey, and Williams) already there. Others claim that the additional men arrived later,

Colonial trace road leading to Kings Mountain. (Kings Mountain National Military Park)

giving rise to more confusion over the final numbers that marched on Kings Mountain.

The Cowpens were owned by a Tory, who was quickly questioned as to the whereabouts of Ferguson. He truthfully replied that the Loyalists had not passed through and, after a search, the Patriots were satisfied he was being honest. A meal of freshly slaughtered beef and corn from the surrounding fields then raised spirits among the tired men.

More encouragement came in the shape of Joseph Kerr, a disabled man who had been able to infiltrate Ferguson's camp when he was only six miles from Kings Mountain. Kerr's report, which confirmed much of what the earlier spy had said, convinced the Patriots that they were close to catching their quarry. After sending out new spies to see if any more intelligence could be gathered (it does not appear that any useful information was found in this way), the Patriots saddled up again at 2100hrs.

Once again, those whose horses had weakened were left behind and around 900 men, on the strongest horses, were selected to start the final push to catch Ferguson. Some sources claim that was the full number that engaged at the ensuing battle, while others claim that the South Carolinians were in addition to that number, rather than included. The most forensic research into the question of Patriot numbers at Kings Mountain has been performed by Bobby Gilmer Moss, who undertook an exhaustive study of official records, including pension applications. His research allowed him to positively identify more than 870 men who were almost certainly at the battle, as well as another 1,200 who may have been either in the battle or on the campaign. Moss' research has been picked up by others, with a consensus developing that around 1,100 Patriots were probably at the battle, with that number possibly rising to around 1,400. An interesting element is the fact that there was a disproportionate number of officers in the force, and analysis of the make-up of the units involved in the battle reveals quite startling facts. In Virginia's Washington County Regiment, for instance, around 50 officers went into the battle at the head of around 100 NCOs and privates. Some estimates suggest that in the total force there

Cherokee Ford, where the Patriots crossed the Broad River. (Overmountain Victory National Historic Trail)

were as many as 396 officers (including 232 captains) leading 700 privates. In a couple of especially lopsided units, there may have actually been more captains than privates.

The imbalance is accounted for by the fact that officers would be likely to have the highest quality horses, and the make-up of the army that fought at Kings Mountain would account for the unusually high proportion of officers among the casualty list after the battle. Early writings suggested that this was due to the bravery of the Patriot officers, who had "led from the front," but it was simply a function of the peculiar imbalance in the units as they went into battle.

The honed-down Patriot force marched through a dark and unpleasant night. Rain was continuous and heavy at times, and the men were forced to keep their rifles dry at the expense of themselves, wrapping clothing around the precious firearms.

The Virginians under Campbell (who was still nominally in overall command) strayed off the correct route to Kings Mountain and had to be rounded up the following morning. After crossing the Broad River at Cherokee Ford, they took a short break at one of Ferguson's previous resting places. Some of the men had food with them, others did not, and the mood was dour following the long and unpleasant night. As they rode past a cornfield, many men grabbed ears of corn for both themselves and their horses.

The likely crossing and dismounting point at Kings Creek, as the Patriots made their final approach to the battlefield. (Kings Mountain National Military Park)

Even though only the strongest animals had been chosen for this final push, some were now breaking down or falling with exhaustion. Warned of this, Shelby is alleged to have replied, "I will not stop until night, if I follow Ferguson into Cornwallis' lines."

Two captured Tories were then impressed to guide the way over the final miles, but there was still the possibility that Ferguson may have moved in the meantime. It would have been the obvious thing to do given his desire to link up with the main army under Cornwallis.

Surprisingly, Ferguson's command was not on the move at the time. Allaire's diary includes no entries for October 4–5, indicating that they did not move at all on those days. On Friday, October 6, he noted that they were under way early, breaking camp at 0400hrs and marching 16 miles to "Little King's Mountain," where they were still encamped the following day.

An element of pride may well have been factored into Ferguson's decision-making at this point, and this is reinforced by a comment in one of his last messages to Cornwallis. On October 5, he wrote that the Patriots had been joined by yet more men and had become "an object of some consequence." He insisted that, "I should still hope for success against them myself; but numbers compared, that must be doubtful." Once more there was a plea for reinforcements ("3 or 400 good soldiers, part dragoons, would finish the business"), but he then added a remarkable request, given the circumstances: "If your Lordship should be pleas'd not to supersede me by sending a superior officer, it will be an addition to the obligations I owe you."

Ferguson was caught between wanting to prove the effectiveness of his Loyalists and the need for support, and whatever factors influenced his erratic movements in the days before the battle, they played right into the Patriots' hands.

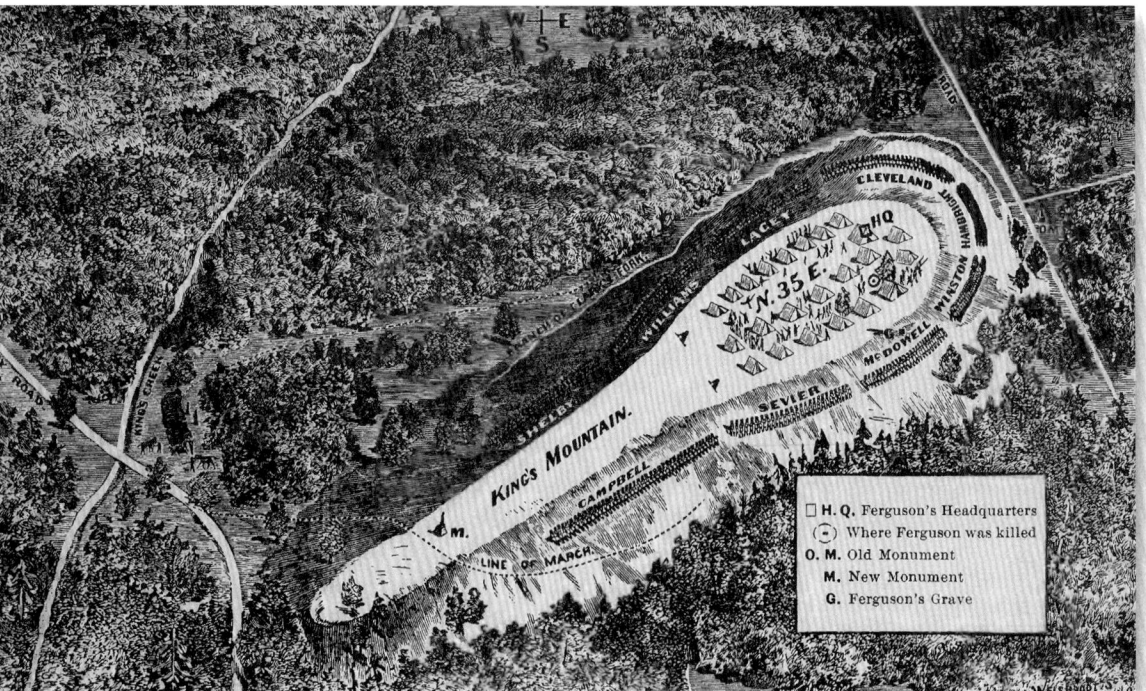

"Diagram of the Battle of King's Mountain." Note that sources disagree on precise troop dispositions at the battle. (From *King's Mountain and its Heroes* by Lyman Draper)

A view of "the Pinnacle," the dominant feature of the Kings Mountain range. (From *King's Mountain and its Heroes* by Lyman Draper)

He had approached the mountain by marching between Buffalo and Kings Creeks, and once he saw the position, he apparently had a change of heart. Having previously said he was marching to join Cornwallis, he wrote again, on October 6, with details of a new plan.

"I arrived to day at King Mountain," he wrote, in what was to be his last letter to his commanding officer, "and have taken up a post where I do not think I can be forced by a stronger enemy than that against us."

Ferguson noted that he had asked Colonel Floyd to come to him with his Loyalists the next day (contradicting the sentiment of his letter to Gibbs), and believed this would give him enough men to act offensively. He hedged his bets, however, claiming only that he would be willing to attack "if you are pleas'd to order us forward." Expecting orders on a tactical level from Cornwallis was unrealistic and suggested an attempt to cover himself if he was later accused of a lack of martial ardor. His final comment would appear pathetic in retrospect. Having said he would be willing to advance if ordered to do so, he added, "but help so near at hand, it appear'd to me improper of myself to commit any thing to hasard."

There was no help at hand. Ferguson would face the Patriots with no reinforcements.

THE BATTLE

The area around the Kings Mountain battlefield is dominated by the Pinnacle, but the battle took place at a far less imposing site six miles away. A rocky outcrop rising to about 60ft above the surrounding territory, it took the form of a 600-yard-long ridge with steep sides, running from northeast to southwest. At its southwesterly tip it is narrow, no more than 60 yards or so in width, but it expands to double that width at the opposite end.

The position instantly appealed to Ferguson. After the battle, one of his Loyalists spoke to a Patriot and stated that, "The situation of King's Mountain was so pleasing that he [Ferguson] concluded to take post there, stoutly affirming that he would be able to destroy or capture any force the Whigs could bring against him."

There was a water supply, a spring on the northwest slope, but the ground was unsuitable for the digging of trenches. Ferguson therefore threw up no defensive works on the summit, ignoring the plentiful supply of wood on the slopes around his position, perhaps feeling that nature had already made his position strong enough, or perhaps simply not anticipating a battle.

In truth, although he had the advantage of high ground, the position was inherently dangerous, especially considering the composition of the force moving against him. A conventional army would have struggled on the wooded slopes, but the Overmountain Men were used to tracking and hunting in forests. The terrain was perfect for their skills and would allow them to move from one piece of cover to the next without unduly exposing themselves to their enemy.

The slope on which provincial and Patriot troops clashed. (Kings Mountain National Military Park)

"Charge of the American frontiersmen," by William Henry Drake. (From *Hero Tales from American History* by Henry Cabot Lodge and Theodore Roosevelt)

Ferguson established his headquarters at the northeast tip of the ridge. He was about 35 miles from Charlotte and could have been halfway there before the Patriots arrived had he not waited, so there is uncertainty over his purpose. If he was inviting an attack, why did he not prepare defensive works? If he was not, why did he linger when it would have made more sense to push on to Charlotte and safety? Even the possibility of his awaiting reinforcements is not straightforward, given his letter to Gibbs warning him to keep away. One final possibility is that he thought the position was too strong to be attacked, and was merely resting his men before setting off again, either to pursue the Patriots or make his way to Charlotte, but his men had been inactive on the 4th and 5th and should not have been unduly tired by a 16-mile march on the 6th.

As well as confusion over the numbers of Patriots at Kings Mountain, it is not clear how many of Ferguson's men were present. His numbers are generally estimated at around 1,100, but there is some evidence that a body of men, perhaps as many as 200, was absent, either foraging or scouting. Overall, however, it seems reasonable to conclude that the Patriots enjoyed a slight advantage in numbers, but nothing near as great as would be claimed by some sources.

As the Patriots made their final approach, two more guides are credited with helping them. A Loyalist household would not offer any details of Ferguson's presence, but one of the daughters is then credited with leaving the house and asking the Patriots how many of them there were.

PATRIOT
1. Sevier
2. Shelby
3. Williams
4. Cleveland
5. Chronicle
6. Winston
7. Joseph McDowell
8. Campbell

Campbell

EVENTS

1. The Patriots split their forces into four groups (two columns of two subsections).

2. Two of the groups envelop the southwestern tip of the ridge, and this is where the fighting breaks out.

3. The second group in the left column loses its way in swampy ground and is unable to take up its final position before the fighting begins.

4. Likewise, men under Winston in the right column initially advance up the wrong slope and also miss the start of the battle.

5. Fierce fighting breaks out between the provincial soldiers under Allaire and the Patriots attacking the southwestern tip of the ridge. Several bayonet charges temporarily force the Patriots to withdraw, but they quickly return to the attack.

6. About 10 minutes after the battle begins, the final Patriot units arrive to envelop the northeastern tip of the ridge and begin to advance.

7. Under intense pressure, and with losses mounting, Allaire's provincials withdraw to the main body, where a final stand is made.

8. Ferguson is shot trying to break out of the encirclement. Fighting continues for some time but the Loyalists are eventually forced to surrender.

THE BATTLE OF KINGS MOUNTAIN, OCTOBER 7, 1780

After tracking Ferguson down, the Patriot militia lose no time in launching a devastating and overwhelming attack on his position.

LOYALIST
A. Allaire (provincials)
B. Ferguson
C. Final Loyalist position

Note: the base map covers an area of approximately 0.9 x 0.6 miles (1.5 × 1km).

Hand-to-hand fighting during the battle. (Kings Mountain National Military Park)

"Enough to whip Ferguson if we can find him," was the reply, at which point the girl pointed and said, "He is on that mountain." If this story is true, the girl must simply have pointed in the general direction of Ferguson's position – from a distance of three miles the actual spot of the battle would have been invisible in the trees and would not have looked anything like a mountain.

More intelligence was given by another girl, questioned by a Patriot spy, who claimed to have taken chickens to Ferguson's camp. Her description of the position, an old deer-hunter's campsite, was so accurate it was recognized by two of the Patriot officers, who claimed they had camped there before. Ferguson's whereabouts had finally been pinpointed.

Just before the engagement, one further piece of information fell into their hands when they were able to capture a messenger from Ferguson, on his way to Cornwallis at Charlotte. The messenger, John Ponder, was just 14 years old, and the letter he carried was another request for reinforcements. He also revealed that Ferguson was wearing a checked hunting shirt over his uniform. The long march was not to have been in vain after all.

Upon reaching Kings Mountain, the Patriots assessed the situation and agreed on a simple but deadly approach. They would entirely surround Ferguson's position and then close in. This was not to be an attempt to shift him from a strong defensive position, again casting doubt on Ferguson's choice of location for a stand. It was a straightforward effort to completely annihilate his command.

Most of the Patriots dismounted, probably near Kings Creek about a mile and half from the battleground, with officers remaining on their horses. They then divided their force into two columns, each comprising two further subsections, each designated to approach the Loyalists from a different direction. It is important to note that these were men who were unused to following orders and unaccustomed to organized military operations, and yet they carried out the plan with surprising efficiency.

Inevitably, there are discrepancies among the eyewitness accounts, but there is no doubt that the two columns surrounded the ridge upon which Ferguson was situated. Campbell and Sevier led their men in the right column, while Shelby and Cleveland commanded on the left. The original plan was probably to wait until the ridge had been completely surrounded before opening the attack, but this would have been difficult for trained troops to accomplish and in the event the attack was launched before all of the Patriots were in position.

The two columns split into their four sections on the final approach, aiming to fold around both the northeastern end of the ridge and southwestern tip. Many of the men removed their hats at this point, tying handkerchiefs around their heads to minimize the risk of getting caught up in branches on their move up the hill, and there is mention of the use of pieces of white paper tucked into headgear to minimize the risk of friendly fire.

The men marching under Winston, as part of the right wing, apparently lost their way on their long flanking march and actually began to climb the wrong ridge before they were informed of their mistake. Hastily withdrawing, they moved off again in search of their true destination, which was still a mile or so away.

Meanwhile, the two center groups, targeting the southwesterly tip of the ridge, inevitably reached their goal first. There is confusion over the exact alignment of the various corps, with a roughly equal number of accounts asserting that either Sevier or Campbell formed the right-center column. It seems likely that Sevier's corps, being the smaller, was assigned to the right-center of the formation, with Campbell's larger corps wrapping around the remainder of the mountain. Nevertheless, it appears that men in Campbell's corps may have been the first to make contact with the enemy.

Joseph Starnes, a private serving under William Campbell, reported that he was with a group of men who either captured or more likely killed a Loyalist picket on the approach to the mountain. The man was taken "without a voice," meaning that he had been unable to raise any sort of alarm. Another picket was then shot by one of Starnes' comrades, at which point any need for stealth was gone. Starnes recounted that Campbell's men then began to advance rapidly.

This fits into many of the accounts of the battle, which assert that the fighting started in this area before the two flanking groups had completed their marches. The response was audible before it was visible. Drums could be heard alerting Ferguson's troops to prepare for action, and some men reported hearing the shrill blasts of Ferguson's whistle.

THE CHARGE OF THE PROVINCIALS AT KINGS MOUNTAIN, OCTOBER 7, 1780 (PP.76–77)

Patrick Ferguson had patiently drilled his men in the tactics of professional soldiery, and although the Loyalist militia would not have been especially proficient, given their limited experience, the provincial soldiers were more accomplished. The men of the various units (including the American Volunteers, the King's American Regiment, the New Jersey Volunteers, the Loyal American Regiment, the Prince of Wales American Regiment, and the King's Carolina Rangers Regiment) gathered together in his small army were skilled in the use of the bayonet and disciplined enough to charge when ordered.

The combination of a determined charge and the flashing of bayonets was nearly always enough to make militia turn tail and run, at least temporarily **(1)**. At Kings Mountain, several charges by the provincials had the desired effect of scattering the Patriots, but the relief did not last long – they were steady enough to return to the fray as soon as the charge had run its course.

It is believed that Lieutenant Anthony Allaire, Ferguson's aide de camp, took part in at least the first charge, on horseback. He is described as confronting one of the Patriot officers and, having the benefit of being mounted, cut him down with a single sword stroke **(2)**. In an account of the battle by Ensign Robert Campbell, he described how the Virginians "obstinately stood until some of them were thrust through the body, and having nothing but their rifles by which to defent themselves, they were forced to retreat" **(3)**.

With most of the provincials on foot, however, it was possible for the Patriots to simply retire to a safe distance and only those who were slow to react were caught out. Casualties inflicted by the charges were therefore low, despite their terrifying appearance, while the Patriots were able to whittle down the number of provincials, firing from cover before retiring **(4)**.

The first concerted firing of the battle appears to have come from Ferguson's men, who must have been quick to respond to their orders. Shelby reported taking fire while his men were still moving into position, one man grumbling that it was humiliating to be receiving fire without returning it. Shelby allegedly replied: "press on to your places, and then your fire will not be lost."

The Patriots had been told to wait until the two groups with the furthest distance to cover had completed their marches, which they would signal by raising a war whoop, but Campbell was unable to contain himself. With the instruction to "shout like hell and fight like devils!" he urged his men forward into the attack. The cries that went up, though not yet from the full strength of the Patriots, carried to the Loyalist troops, where DePeyster is reported to have said "These are the damned yelling boys," his mind going back to Musgrove Mill.

Colonel Cleveland, in the Patriots' left wing, was slowed by a patch of waterlogged land, but as he finally approached the mountain he is credited with a lengthy speech to his men, delivered from horseback. The gist of the speech was not to break if repulsed, but to return to the fray. They had been delayed by as much as 10 minutes by the swampy ground, and the fight was in full swing by the time they arrived.

DePeyster mentioned a bayonet charge from the provincials in the Loyalist force, and this would have been a terrifying prospect for the Patriots. Although the provincials under Ferguson's command numbered no more than 100 (and it is not clear how many were engaged in this charge), it was effective, scattering the Patriots and sending them headlong back down the hill. This first charge is believed to have taken place against Virginians under Campbell, but DePeyster reported that Ferguson, believing the absence of his steadiest soldiers on the ridge might cause the rest of his men to break, quickly recalled the provincials.

Things appear to have deteriorated on the Loyalist side from that moment. DePeyster reported that the retreat of the provincials caused confusion and alarm among the Loyalist militia, who did not understand why they had been recalled and thought they had been beaten back. It is more likely, however, that DePeyster was conflating events in his report, understandably muddled by the confusion of the battle. Most sources describe two or three bayonet charges, and it is likely that the breakdown in discipline described by DePeyster only occurred after the losses suffered in repeated charges at the enemy. His report stated that only a few of the Loyalists were standing at their posts, and that those from the district of Ninety Six were proving the steadiest. Even these men, however, panicked when the provincials withdrew, prompting some to give up the fight or attempt to flee, as indicated by DePeyster noting that "the officers cut some of them down."

The bayonet charges, though effective, had provided only a brief respite. The panicking Loyalist militia appear to have infected even the provincials, as DePeyster reported that "they [the militia] broke us in such a manner that we could no longer act." He estimated having just 22 men left out of his provincial corps, strongly suggesting that this was after multiple charges and not just the single charge mentioned in his report.

On the Patriot side, the Virginians had been panicked by the first charge, running up the slopes of the next ridge to escape the dreaded

Ferguson is depicted falling from his horse during his final charge towards the Patriot militia. (From *King's Mountain and its Heroes* by Lyman Draper)

bayonets, but they were steadied by their officers and returned to advance again. Shelby would not have been able to see events at such a distance from his own position (most maps of the battle have the ridge between his men and Campbell's). Nonetheless, he later reported, "On the first onset, the Washington militia attempted rapidly to ascend the mountain, but were met by the British regulars with fixed bayonets, and forced to retreat. They were soon rallied by their gallant commander, and some of his active officers, and by a constant and well-directed fire of our rifles we drove them back in our turn, and reached the summit of the mountain."

The fighting was escalating as the Patriots made their way up the slopes. One resonant phrase from John Haywood, one of many historians to have written about the battle, stands out: "The mountain was covered with flame and smoke, and seemed to thunder."

Shelby mentioned rallying his men after another repulse in the face of a bayonet charge, shouting, "Now, boys, quickly re-load your rifles, and let's advance upon them, and give them another hell of a fire!" Such words would have been ironic, as the rifles carried by his men were not quick to reload. On an open plain, Ferguson's Loyalists, armed with muskets and trained to fire in volleys, would have had the upper hand, being able to get off three or four shots for every one fired in return by a rifleman. On the slopes of Kings Mountain, the slower rate of fire for the rifles was not an issue, as the men could safely take cover while reloading, and only the occasional bayonet charge gave them much cause for concern.

Many accounts of the battle mention the Loyalists on top of the ridge being drawn up in dense formations, making tempting targets for the

Another depiction of the fall of Patrick Ferguson by Alonzo Chappel (1863). (Prints, Drawings and Watercolors from the Anne S. K. Brown Military Collection, Brown Digital Repository, Brown University Library)

Patriot riflemen. Many also mention volley fire from Ferguson's men, which would have created a spectacle but would have been ineffective against men advancing in skirmish order and moving from one piece of cover to the next. Similar (justified) comments were made about the performance of Edward Braddock's army at the Battle of the Monongahela, back in 1755, but the British Army had learned a lot about fighting in North America since then. Ferguson's specialty was light infantry tactics rather than the dense formations of the regular infantry, and he had drilled his men thoroughly. Volley fire would undoubtedly have been part of their training, but it is highly unlikely that he would have employed that tactic exclusively on Kings Mountain. It seems more likely that an initial volley, intended to impress the Patriots, would have been followed by more independent fire. It is also likely that an 'open' order was utilized by his men rather than the packed lines adopted by regular infantry in standard battlefield tactics of the time. Even so, the Loyalists did not have the same sort of cover to work behind. The crest of the ridge was largely free from trees, and their casualties began to mount.

After about 10 minutes of fighting around the southwestern tip of the ridge, the remainder of the Patriot force was able to engage. Lacey, attacking the northeastern flank of the ridge, had his horse shot out from under him as soon as he began to move up the slope. On the northeast slope, the steepest of them all, Hambright and Chronicle led their men into battle. Chronicle, leading from the front, fell to a musket ball, apparently immediately after exhorting his men to "face the hill!" Captain John Mattocks and Lieutenants William Rabb and John Boyd also died in this

Ferguson's second-in-command, DePeyster, is shown surrendering to Patriot forces in this woodcut from an original illustration by Charles Stanley Reinhart. (Ivy Close Images/Alamy)

volley, and Hambright suffered a severe wound, his boot filling with blood from a shot taken in the thigh.

It is clear that another bayonet charge was faced in this sector. Robert Henry, a 15-year-old in Chronicle's group, found himself on the sharp end, a bayonet piercing his hand and entering his thigh, although he seems to have managed to fire his rifle at the last moment, wounding the man attacking him. Henry then had to endure the trial of having the bayonet pulled out of his thigh, and a friend had to kick at his hand to free it from

The battlefield marker stone commemorating the spot where Ferguson fell in battle. (Kings Mountain National Military Park)

the blade. Henry survived, but his assailant was bleeding heavily and almost certainly did not.

The battle had developed into a series of small-scale combats. In one account, Thomas Young (a major though only 16 years of age) described how he and a comrade moved up the ridge:

> Ben Hollingworth and myself took right up the side of the mountain, and fought our way from tree to tree, up to the summit. I recollect I stood behind one tree and fired until the bark was nearly all knocked off, and my eyes pretty well filled with it. One fellow shaved me pretty close, for his bullet took a piece out of my gun stock. Before I was aware of it, I found myself apparently between my own regiment and the enemy, as I judged from seeing the paper the Whigs wore in their hats, and the pine twigs the Tories wore in theirs, these being the badges of distinction.

When the wings of the Patriot force engaged, Ferguson's men realized they were surrounded and steadily gave ground, gathering at the northeastern end of the ridge, where the plateau was wider. Amid the confusion, word began to spread through the Patriots that Tarleton had arrived with his Legion to save the day for Ferguson, but no such rescue was at hand. At around this time, James Williams was shot, and the controversial officer would die the next day. Such was the animosity towards him that there were rumors that he had actually been shot by a Patriot, an early example of "fragging," but this is debated.

As the ground occupied by the Loyalist forces shrank, Ferguson was visibly and audibly active as he moved from one point to another on horseback while also issuing blasts on his whistle. The fighting spirit was going out of his men, however, and he is reported as having to knock down white flags of surrender in various parts of his lines.

Then, when attempting to break through the Patriots in a desperate bid to escape, Ferguson was shot and slowly fell from the saddle, although one foot remained in its stirrup. Many Patriots would later claim to have fired the fatal shot and although this is common in such circumstances, in this case many of them might have been telling the truth – the news that he was wearing a checked hunting shirt had been circulated and the Patriots would have recognized the officer on horseback. He was hit at least six times. Major Archibald McArthur later wrote to Ferguson's family, claiming that had Ferguson not fallen, his men would likely have won the day, but that was merely to give comfort to a grieving family – the outcome of the battle was already beyond all doubt, although resistance continued for a short while.

Legend has it that the resting place of Ferguson was originally beneath the "Tory Tulip Tree." (From *King's Mountain and its Heroes* by Lyman Draper)

Kings Mountain National Military Park, with Ferguson's grave visible in the middle distance. (CC BY 3.0 via Wikimedia Commons)

More white flags of surrender began to appear and now there was nobody to tear them down, but for a while the Patriots refused to accept any surrender. John Sevier's own son, believing his father to have been killed, refused to stop firing until his father appeared to prove he was still alive, and William Campbell made strenuous efforts to restrain his men, insisting it was murder to continue the killing. Finally, the shooting died away, and the battle was over. It had lasted around an hour and almost all of Ferguson's command had been killed, wounded, or captured.

The Patriots had suffered fewer than 100 casualties in securing their complete victory. They had lost 28 killed and 64 wounded while Ferguson's losses had been far more substantial. The Loyalists had seen 157 die, 163 wounded, and almost 700 taken prisoner. The disparity in casualty numbers has led some historians to conclude that the Loyalists made the common mistake, when firing downhill, of overshooting their target. It is equally likely to have been the result of the superior cover available to the Patriots, and their skillful use of it. Whatever the reason, it was a stunning victory, and its repercussions would quickly be felt.

AFTERMATH

On October 8, Cornwallis wrote to Ferguson, unaware that the Inspector of Loyalist Militia had died the day before, and that his command had ceased to exist. There was a hint of testiness in response to Ferguson's appeal for orders in his letter of October 5 – "it appears to me to depend on their [the Patriots'] situation," Cornwallis reasonably pointed out. "Of this you take no notice." Having asserted that he could not be expected to give orders to attack if he did not know what the full situation was, he proceeded to give news about enemy movements around Charlotte and lamented that "we are now surrounded by vast numbers of militia."

The move into North Carolina, delayed and tentative as it already was, had been dealt a serious blow at Kings Mountain, but it would be several days before the British general learned of it. In the meantime, he felt confident

Nathanael Greene (left) takes command of the Southern Army from Horatio Gates in this illustration by Howard Pyle. (From *The Story of the Revolution* by Henry Cabot Lodge via Library of Congress)

Colonel Washington (left) clashes with Banastre Tarleton in "Battle of the Cowpens." (Classic Collection 3/Alamy)

enough to sign off with the following words: "I shall order McArthur to join me here, as I now consider you perfectly safe."

It was three days later before DePeyster was able to write, and he made several mentions of the fact that he was being watched while he did so, and that the letter would be read by the Patriots before it was sent, meaning he could not give out any potentially useful information. DePeyster gave a fairly balanced report on the chaotic battle, although he inaccurately suggested that the Loyalists had been badly outnumbered.

"Their numbers enabl'd them to surround our post," he wrote, "and ours was only sufficient to form a single line on top of the hill." DePeyster went on to suggest that it was unsteadiness among the militia that had been their undoing.

Many of those militiamen faced a grisly end. As well as the dead, significant numbers had been too severely wounded to be moved from the field, so they simply remained there until they passed away. In many cases their remains were eaten by wild animals. The close to 700 men taken prisoner could consider themselves lucky, but their ordeal was not yet over. A few days after they were marched away, William Campbell issued a telling order, asking his officers to prevent his men from "slaughtering and disturbing the prisoners."

A hastily organized trial condemned 30 of the prisoners to death. Presumably men who had previously enlisted in the Patriot militia, they were to face the same justice meted out by Thomas Brown in Augusta the previous month. Nine of the prisoners were duly hanged, but the rest were pardoned.

Banastre Tarleton, no doubt chafing at missing out on the action for so long, finally returned to the saddle on October 10, and was instantly dispatched to assist Ferguson, but he soon heard the news and also a rumor that Ferguson's body had been subjected to "every insult and indignity" after he had died, although there is no contemporary evidence that anyone urinated on his body, as was reported by some.

The British offensive into North Carolina was severely weakened by the loss of Ferguson's 1,000-strong corps. Meant to keep Cornwallis' flank clear, he had instead been overwhelmed and totally destroyed by the very men he was supposed to keep at arm's length. Considering the dire situation in Charlotte, where the British found themselves under constant harassment from a hostile local population, it was clear that Cornwallis' hopes had been misplaced – he had no choice but to drastically rethink his options. The loss of Ferguson had removed the shield protecting his left flank and a large Patriot force was now operating in his rear. On October 12, he withdrew his forces from Charlotte.

In January 1781, the British position was further undone by the comprehensive beating taken by Tarleton at the Battle of Cowpens. It was a

The collapse of the British position in the South, 1781

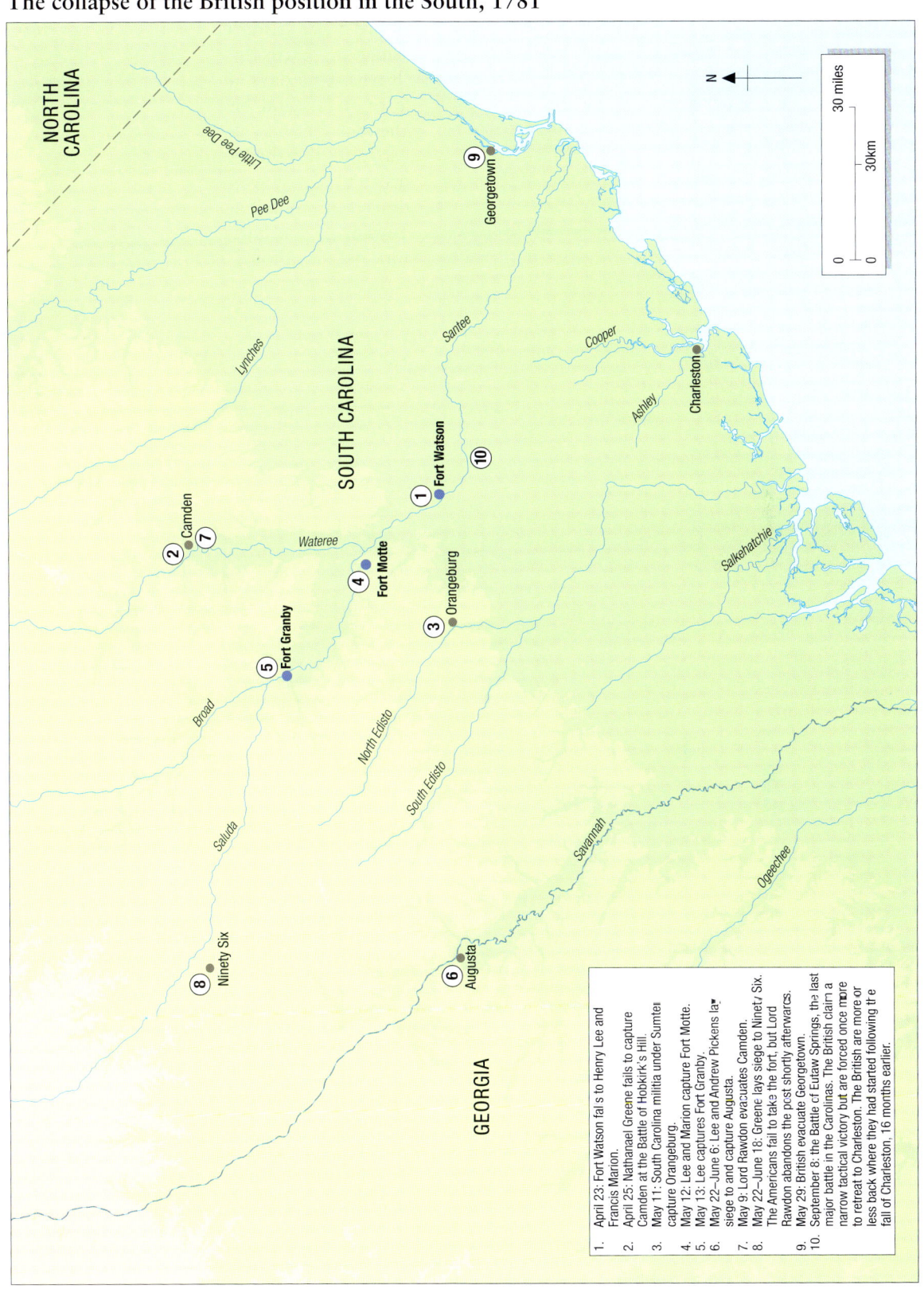

defeat on a similar scale to that of Kings Mountain, with almost every one of Tarleton's 1,150 men killed, wounded, or captured.

The twin defeats, coming in such quick succession, were hammer blows to the British cause in the South. In both instances, Patriot militia had proved how effective they could be against British regulars, provincials, and Loyalist militia alike.

The loss of Ferguson's corps was arguably the less severe of the two blows. A Loyalist militia force could be reformed, while the regulars and provincials under Tarleton were irreplaceable. Even so, the defeat at Kings Mountain marked a turning point in the South. Patriot fortunes had been at their lowest following the string of triumphs that had seen the British take a firm grip on South Carolina and Georgia, but Kings Mountain instilled fresh confidence and vigor. Cornwallis' strategy was not exactly in tatters. Even after the defeat of Tarleton, he remained committed to his North Carolina offensive and relaunched it in 1781, but the road he took led only to Yorktown.

In the late 19th century, a romantic postscript was given to the story of Kings Mountain when the grave of Ferguson was allegedly excavated. The work was done by a local doctor with no archaeological training and two bodies were found in it, one of which was female. There is a story that Ferguson had two camp women with him at the time of the battle, one of whom, "Virginia Sal," had been killed while helping with the wounded during the battle.

It is a nice story, but, as with many elements of this battle, it is disputed. It is unclear whether these two camp women actually existed, and it is also a flip of the coin as to whether or not the grave in question was actually Ferguson's, but who would deny the British officer a little company in the two and a half centuries since he fell?

THE BATTLEFIELD TODAY

The Kings Mountain battlefield is beautifully preserved as part of the Kings Mountain National Military Park (not to be confused with the Kings Mountain State Park, which is only about three miles away). This is the only battlefield of the Revolutionary War preserved in its entirety and it is part of a string of parks (the Southern Campaign of the American Revolution Parks in South Carolina) that also includes Cowpens National Battlefield, Ninety Six National Historic Site, and the Overmountain Victory National Historic Trail. Together, they offer the chance to experience in great detail the geography of the campaign.

The battlefield monument in the Kings Mountain National Military Park, situated on the site of the Loyalist encampment. (NPS/Victoria Stauffenberg)

The headstone of Patrick Ferguson's grave (note that it is not certain that this is his actual resting place). (CC BY 3.0 via Wikimedia Commons)

At Kings Mountain, a mile-and-a-half trail has been created to take you around the battle site, including along the ridge where the Loyalist forces made their stand and were overwhelmed. Although steep in some places, the path has been paved and is suitable for wheelchair users.

There are over a dozen monuments, memorials, and markers in the park. For the battlefield enthusiast, the most important are the US Monument (which marks the site of the Loyalist encampment where the battle ended), the grave of Patrick Ferguson (on the spot traditionally said to be his burial site), and the Chronicle Marker (commemorating Major William Chronicle). The park also features a visitors' center, with various exhibits and artifacts related to the battle and its participants, including an original Ferguson rifle.

Each year, on the weekend closest to the anniversary of the battle, the park hosts a large commemorative event, when many descendants of the men who participated in the battle make pilgrimages to the park. You can find out more information at: www.nps.gov/kimo/index.htm

The route followed by the Overmountain Men on their march to the battle has been preserved as the Overmountain Victory National Historic Trail. This 330-mile-long trail was created to protect the route and share the unique story of when the people of Appalachia changed the course of the American Revolution. While it is primarily a commemorative motor route, partners along the corridor continue to expand a network of hiking trails that follow the route. You can find out more information about the trail at: www.nps.gov/ovvi/index.htm

A stone monument in the park bears a plaque with a brief description of the fateful battle. (NPS/Victoria Stauffenberg)

Diorama of the battle in the visitors' center. (Kings Mountain National Military Park)

The original Chronicle marker, the second-oldest battlefield memorial in the United States, erected in 1814 alongside the replacement marker erected in 1914. (Kings Mountain National Military Park)

SELECT BIBLIOGRAPHY

PRINTED PRIMARY SOURCES

Allaire, A., "Diary of Lieut. Anthony Allaire," in Draper, L. C., *King's Mountain and its Heroes*, New York: Dauber & Pine Bookshops Inc. (1929)
Hanger, G., *The Life and Opinions of Col. George Hanger*, London: J. DeBrett (1801)
Moss, B. G. (ed.), *Journal of Capt. Alexander Chesney: Adjutant to Maj. Patrick Ferguson*, Blacksburg, SC: Scotia-Hibernia Press (2002)
Ross, C. (ed.), *Correspondence of Charles, First Marquis Cornwallis, Vol. I*, London: John Murray (1859)
Saberton, I. (ed.), *The Cornwallis Papers: The Campaigns of 1780 and 1781 in The Southern Theatre of the American Revolutionary War, Vols. I and II*, Uckfield, UK: The Naval & Military Press (2010)
Stevens, B. F. (ed.), *The Campaign in Virginia 1781: An Exact Reprint of Six Rare Pamphlets on the Clinton–Cornwallis Controversy* (1888)

SECONDARY SOURCES

Boatner, M. M., *Encyclopedia of the American Revolution*, Mechanicsburg, PA: Stackpole Books (1994)
Dykeman, W., *With Fire and Sword: The Battle of Kings Mountain 1780*, Washington DC: National Park Service (1978)
Ferguson, A., *Biographical Sketch or Memoir of Lieutenant-Colonel Patrick Ferguson*, Edinburgh: John Moir (1817)
Fortescue, J. W., *A History of the British Army, First Part to the Close of the Seven Years' War, Vol. II*, London: Macmillan and Co. (1899)
Gilchrist, M. M., *Patrick Ferguson: A Man of Some Genius*, Leeds, UK: NMS Publishing (2003)
Kirkland, T. J. and Kennedy, R. M., *Historic Camden: Part One – Colonial and Revolutionary*, Columbia, SC: The State Company (1905)
Landrum, J. B. O., *Colonial and Revolutionary History of Upper South Carolina*, Greenville, SC: Shannon & Co. (1897)
Lathan, R., *Historical Sketch of the Battle of King's Mountain*, Yorkville, SC: The Enquirer (1880)
Moss, B. G., *The Patriots at Kings Mountain*, Blacksburg, SC: Scotia-Hibernia Press (1990)
Moss, B. G., *The Loyalists at Kings Mountain*, Blacksburg, SC: Scotia-Hibernia Press (1998)
O'Kelley, P., *Nothing but Blood and Slaughter: The Revolutionary War in the Carolinas, Vol. Two: 1780*, Lillington, NC: Blue House Tavern Press (2004)
Spring, M. H., *With Zeal and with Bayonets Only: The British Army on Campaign in North America, 1775–1783*, Norman, OK: University of Oklahoma Press (2010)
Wickwire, F. and M., *Cornwallis and the War of Independence*, London: Faber & Faber (1970)
Willcox, W. B. (ed.), *The American Rebellion: Sir Henry Clinton's Narrative*, New Haven: Yale University Press (1954)

JOURNAL PAPERS

Caldwell, W., "Isaac Shelby, Patrick Ferguson, and Fire & Sword: The Power of a Good Story," *Journal of the American Revolution* (May 28, 2024)

Dorney, D. R., "An Imprudent and Unnecessary Measure: Major Problems in the First Invasion of North Carolina, September–October 1780," *Journal of the Society for Army Historical Research*, Vol. 99 (2021), pp. 152–69

Piecuch, J., "The Battle of Kings Mountain: New Insights from Forgotten Documents," *Journal of the American Revolution* (September 12, 2024)

Rauch, S. J., "Southern (Dis)Comfort: British Phase IV Operations in South Carolina and Georgia, May–September 1780," *Army History*, No. 71 (Spring 2009) pp. 34–50

Robertson, H., "The Second British Occupation of Augusta, 1780–1781," *The Georgia Historical Quarterly*, Vol. 58, No. 4 (Winter 1974), pp. 422–46

Williams, S. C., "The Battle of King's Mountain: As Seen by the British Officers," *Tennessee Historical Magazine*, Vol. 7, No. 1 (April 1921), pp. 51–66

PHD THESIS

Mabelitini, C. B., "British Fortification Strategy in the South Carolina Backcountry During the Southern Campaign of the American Revolution." University of South Carolina (2024)

INDEX

Figures in **bold** refer to illustrations.

Adair, John 53
Alexander's Ford **64**
Allaire, Lieutenant Anthony 15, 45–46, 56, 62, 68, **76–77**, 78
Augusta 36, 37, 39, 43, 55

backcountry, expansion into **4**, 5
Balfour, Lieutenant Colonel Nisbet 6, 37
battle plans
    Loyalist **22–23**
    Patriot **24**
Beattie's Ford 62–63
blockhouses 35
Blue Savannah 36
Braddock, Edward 81
Bratton, Colonel William 25
Brown, Lieutenant Colonel Thomas 12, 27–28, 36, 39, 43

Camden, Battle of 28, **28**, **29**, 33
camp women 88
campaign details and events 25–84
    chronology 8–9
    Cornwallis' offensive 33–36
    destruction of Gates' Grand Army 28–33
    early events **26**
    Ferguson's campaign, beginning of 43–49
    final reinforcements and preparations 62–69
    Mackay's Trading Post, Siege of 36–43, **38**, **40–41**, **42**
    origins of the campaign 5–8
    Sycamore Shoals muster 49–55, **49**, **50–51**, **52**, **54**, **55**
    see also Kings Mountain, Battle of
Campbell, Colonel William 12, **12**, 53–54, 59, 63, 64–65, 67, 75, 79, 84, 86
Campbell, Ensign Robert 54, 78
casualties and losses 27, 31, 33, 47, 84, 86, 88
Charleston 5, 6, 7, 13, 23, 35, 36, 43
Chronicle, Major William 62, 81, 90
Clarke, Colonel Elijah 13, **13**, 28, 31–32, 36, 39, **40–41**, 42, 46, 55, 60
Cleveland, Colonel Benjamin 16, 58, 59, 63, 75, 79
Clinton, Sir Henry 6, **6**, 7, 10, 14, 34–35
commanders
    Loyalist 10–12
    Patriot 12–13

Cornwallis, Charles, Earl 6–7, **10**, 15, 22–23, 28, 30, 31, 33–36, 44, 45, 53–54, 55, 59, 68, 69, 85–86, **86**, 88
Cornwallis House **30**
Cowpens 64, 65–66, 86, **86**, 89
Cruger, Lieutenant Colonel John 39, 43, 59–60
Cuming, Sir Alexander **37**

Davie, Major William 27
DePeyster, Captain Abraham 11–12, **11**, 15, 33, 46, 79, **82**, 86
Disqualifying Act 1780 39
Dykeman, Wilma 44, 53

fatigue 64
Ferguson, Major Patrick 6–7, 10–11, **11**, 14–16, 22, 23, **24**, 27, 29, 31, 33, 34–35, 43, 43–49, 53–55, 58–59, 62, 63–64, 65–66, 68–69, 70–71, 74–75, 85
    charge of the provincials at King's Mountain **76–77**, 78, 79
    declaration to Patriots 47–49
    fall from horse and death 80, 81, **82**, 83, 84
    Ferguson rifle 10, **44**, **45**
    grave **83**, **84**, 88, 90, **90**
    headquarters 63
Fishing Creek 29–31
Floyd, Colonel 69
fortifications 37, 39, 43

Ganey, Major Micajah 36
Gates, General Horatio 6, 28, **29**, 33, 59, 63, 85
Georgetown 45
Georgia **22**, 27–28, 32, 36, 36–37, 44, 46, 88
Germain, Lord George 29, 33
Gibbs, Colonel Zacharias 65
Graham, Colonel William 62
Greene, Nathanael 85, 87

Hambright, Lieutenant Colonel William 62, 81–82
Hammond, Major Samuel 62, **63**
Hampton, Lieutenant Colonel Wade 46, **46**
Hanger, Major George 5, 54
Hanging Rock 27, **28**
hangings 27–28, 43, 44–45, 86
Hawthorn, Lieutenant Colonel James 62
Haywood, John 80
Henry, Robert 82–83
Hill, Colonel William 62–63, 65
horses 31, 47, **50–51**, 52, 63, 65, 66, 67–68

Howe, Major General William 10–11
Huck, Captain Christian 25

Inman, Captain Shadrack 32
Innes, Lieutenant Colonel Alexander 32, 33, 36
intelligence 23, 30, 42, 46, 48, 54, 56, 64, 66, 71, 74

Kerr, Joseph 66
Kings Creek 67, 69, 75
Kings Mountain, Battle of 11–12, **15**, 16, 48–49, 56, **68**
    aftermath 85–88
    battlefield today 89–92
    British collapse in the South **87**, 88
    charge of the provincials **76–77**, 78, 79
    details of the battle 69–84, **70**, **72–73**, **91**
    hand-to-hand fighting **74**
    Loyalist surrender 84
    marker stones **82**, **92**
    monuments 89, **90**, **91**
    Pinnacle, the 69–71, **69**
    road to **57**, **61**, 65–69, **65**, **67**
    small-scale combats 83
    volley fire 81

Lacey, Colonel Edward 62–63, 64–65, 81
Loyalist forces
    battle plans **22–23**
    commanders 10–12
    illness 35, 44
    order of battle 17–18
Loyalist military units
    7th (Royal) Fusiliers 45
    63rd Regiment 35
    71st Regiment 35
    British Legion 28–29, 30, 44, 56, 58, 83
    Prince of Wales American Regiment 35
Loyalists 25, 27, 31–33, 36, 44–45, 48, 60, 62, 65–66, 80–81, 88
    charge of the provincials at King's Mountain **76–77**, 78, 79
    lack of faith in 34–35
    New Jersey Volunteers 32
    numbers of, at King's Mountain 71
    recruitment and training 34
    South Carolina Royalists 32
    surrender at Kings Mountain 84

McArthur, Major Archibald 83, 86
McDowell, Charles 16, 33, 46–47, 53, 58, 63
McDowell, Major Joseph 59, **60**

Mackay's Trading Post 36–43, **38**, **40–41**, 42
Marion, Francis 35–36, **35**, **36**, 45
militia 5–7, 14–15, 23, 24
    Loyalists 25, 27, 31–33, 33–35, 36, 44–45, 48, 60, 62, 65–66, **76–77**, 78, 79, 80–81, 88
    Patriots 25, 28, **29**, 31–33, 36, 46–48, 55–56, 58–60, 63–66, 79, 81, 82–83, 88
    quality of men 15
    recruitment and training 34
Moncrief, Captain James 45
Monongahela, Battle of 81
Moore's Creek Bridge, Battle of 14, **14**
Moss, Bobby Gilmer 66
Musgrove Hill, Battle of 31–33, **31**

Native Americans 36–37, **37**, 39, 43, 44, 47
Nelson's Ferry 35
Ninety Six 6, 27, 33, 37, **37**, 39, 43, 46, 55, 56, 59, 62, 63
North Carolina 10, 22–23, **22**, 33, 43–44, **58**

Old Iron Works 63, 64, 65
opposing forces
    Loyalist 14–16
    Patriot 16
order of battle
    Loyalist forces 17–18
    Patriot forces 18–21
Overmountain Men 16, 24, 33, 36, 47, 49, **56**, 60, 90
    Sycamore Shoals muster 49–55, **50–51**, **52**, **54**, **55**

partisans 28–29, 35, 36, 45, 46
Paterson, Brigadier General James 36
Patriot forces 16
    battle plans 24
    commanders 12–13
    order of battle 18–21
    Patriots 25, 28, **29**, 31–33, 36, 39, 56, 58–60, 63–66, 74–75, 79, 81, 82–83, 88
    5th Maryland Regiment 29, 30, 31
    declarations to 47–49
    numbers of, at King's Mountain 66–67, 71
    officers 66–67
    Sycamore Shoals muster 49–55, **49**, **50–51**, **52**, **54**, **55**
    Virginia Mountaineers **16**
    Virginians 16, 53, 67, **76–77**, 78, 79–80
    Washington County Regiment of Militia 66
    Wilkes County Militia 29
pickets 75
Ponder, John 74
prisoners of war 28, 29, 31, 33, 35, 43, 47, 84, 86

Quaker Meadows 56, 57, 59, **61**

Ramsour's Mill, Battle of 22, 62
Rawdon, Lord Francis 45, 49
Regulators 43–44
religion 5
Rocky Mount 25, 27
Roebuck, Colonel Benjamin 62

Sevier, Lieutenant Colonel John 12–13, **12**, 16, 53, 75, 84
Shelby, Colonel Isaac 13, **13**, 16, 25, 31–33, 36, 48, 49, 53–54, 56, 58, 59, 62, 63, 68, 75, 79, 80
slavery 5
South Carolina 5, 10, 22–23, **22**, 25, 35, 43, **58**, 88
Starnes, Private Joseph 75
Sumter, Colonel Thomas 25, 27, **27**, 28–30, 31, 62–63
Sycamore Shoals 49–55, **49**, **50–51**, **52**, **54**, **55**

Tarleton, Banastre 25, 27, 28–31, **30**, 44, 86, **86**, 88
Thicketty Fort 25
Turnbull, Lieutenant Colonel 29, **29**

wagon trains **36**
war cries 33, 79
Watauga Association 44
Waxhaws **25**
weapons
    bayonets 32, **32**, **76–77**, 78, 79–80, 82–83
    cannons 31
    muskets 31, **32**, 80
    rifles 10, 16, **24**, 44, 45, 67, 80
Wemyss, Major James 35, 44–45
Williams, Colonel James 31–32, 62–63, 65, 83
Williamson's Plantation, Battle of 25
Winston, Joseph 16, 59, **59**, 75
Wright, Sir James 36, 43

Yorktown 10, 13, 88
Young, Major Thomas 83